8/7 ⑭ ⅄4/16
12/19 1-18 ⅄7/19
'21 ⑲ ↗

CANADIAN

CONCEPTS

Second Edition

5

Lynda Berish

Sandra Thibaudeau

Collège Marie-Victorin

Prentice Hall Allyn and Bacon Canada
Don Mills, Ontario

Canadian Cataloguing in Publication Data

Berish, Lynda, date
  Canadian concepts 5

2nd ed.
ISBN 978-0-13-591728-2

1. English language—Textbooks for second language learners.*
2. English Language—Grammar.   3. English language—Problems,
exercises, etc.   I. Thibaudeau, Sandra, date.   II. Title.

PE1128.B475 1997   428.2'4   C96-931830-8

© Copyright 1998 Prentice-Hall Canada Inc., Don Mills, Ontario
Pearson Education

ALL RIGHTS RESERVED

It is illegal to reproduce any portion of this book except by special
arrangement with the publisher. Reproduction of this material
without authorization, by any duplication process whatsoever,
is a violation of copyright.

Allyn and Bacon, Inc., Needham Heights, Massachusetts
Prentice-Hall, Inc., Upper Saddle River, New Jersey
Prentice-Hall International (UK) Limited, London
Prentice-Hall of Australia, Pty., Ltd., Sydney
Prentice-Hall Hispanoamericana, S. A., Mexico
Prentice-Hall of India Private Limited, New Delhi
Prentice-Hall of Japan, Inc., Tokyo
Prentice-Hall of Southeast Asia (PTE) Ltd., Singapore
Simon & Schuster Asia Private Limited, Singapore
Editora Prentice-Hall do Brasil Ltda., Rio de Janeiro

ISBN 978-0-13-591728-2

Acquisitions editor: Dominique Roberge
Developmental editor: Marta Tomins
Production editor: Elynor Kagan
Editorial assistant: Ivetka Vasil
Production coordinator: Sharon Houston
Design: Monica Kompter
Layout: Joseph Chin
Text illustrations: Heather Collins, Paul McCusker
Unit opening illllustrations: Carole Giguère
Cover image: Ron Watts/First Light, Skyline, False Creek, B.C.,
  Charleston Park Looking North

Printed and bound in Canada

  6789 IG 098

Credits

The authors would like to acknowledge, with thanks, the
organizations, publications, and individuals who gave
permission to reprint articles used in this text.

"The 7-Minute Meal" by Judy Schultz: *Edmonton Journal*,
Southam Newspapers, September 1996. Reprinted with
permission of the *Edmonton Journal*.

"Who Are They Fooling" by Lisa Tant: From "Fashion
Models Hardly Reflect Reality," *Vancouver Sun*. Reprinted
by permission of the author.

"How a Thief Stole My Name" by Marcia Vickers:
Reprinted by permission of the author.

"Medicine: It's Not All the Same": Reprinted from *Dr.
Andrew Weil's Self Healing* (July 1996, page 8), 42 Pleasant
St., Watertown MA 02172. Subscriptions: $29 for 12
issues: (800) 523-3296.

"Suddenly Grown-up" by Dani Shapiro: Reprinted by
permission of International Creative Management, Inc.
Copyright ©1997 by Dani Shapiro.

"Seduced in the Supermarket" by Thomas Hine: From
The Total Package by Thomas Hine. Copyright ©1995 by
Thomas Hine. By permission of Little, Brown and
Company.

"Night Work" by Sandy Bauers: Reprinted by permission of
the Knight-Ridder/Tribune News Service.

We would like to express our appreciation to all the ESL professionals we have had the pleasure of meeting over the past five years for their encouragement and particularly for their thoughtful comments, which have enabled us to bring so many fresh ideas to the second edition of *Canadian Concepts*.

Thanks also to Max and Millicent Goldman and Tara Berish, for proofreading.

CONTENTS

LISTENING ACTIVITIES	VIDEO ACTIVITIES
1. Entering Canada	
2. Experiences in Dining	1. The Pizza Police (2:29 minutes)
3. In the Name of Beauty	
4. Animal Partners	2. Cinnamon Bear (9:15 minutes)
5. Are You a Good Witness?	
6. Why Do You Do That?	3. The *Farmer's Almanac* (7:6 minutes)

LISTENING ACTIVITIES	VIDEO ACTIVITIES
7. Evaluating Alternative Medicine	
8. Becoming an Adult	4. Country Courtin' (7:18 minutes)
9. Watching Your Shopping Habits	5. What's In a Name? (6:8 minutes)
10. Starting a Business	6. Finding Money (6:29 minutes)

TO THE TEACHER

The *Canadian Concepts* Series

The new edition of the popular *Canadian Concepts* series retains the Canadian focus designed to help students feel at home and integrate into the community. In the new edition, exercises and activities have been graded and refocussed to provide a careful build-up of skills throughout the series. *Canadian Concepts 1* is paced to accommodate the needs of post-literacy students. *Canadian Concepts 2* provides a controlled expansion of survival English topics, vocabulary, and structure. *Canadian Concepts 3 and 4* provide the concrete themes necessary to reinforce language while offering a greater challenge in terms of pacing, tasks, and input. Video clips are integrated into the units in *Canadian Concepts 4, 5, and 6.*

The *Canadian Concepts* series uses a communicative approach. The method offers productive strategies for language learning based on student-centred interaction. Many new activities, games, and opportunities for speaking have been incorporated into the series to encourage maximum student participation in classroom activities. The pedagogical model presents students with challenging listening or reading input, leading them through pre-activities and strategies that make the input comprehensible. In addition to these fluency-building activities, dictation, grammar, spelling, and vocabulary work focus on improving students' accuracy.

Canadian Concepts 5

Canadian Concepts 5 departs from the concrete focus of the previous levels and introduces more controversial, opinion-based topics. Activities challenge students to deal with stimulating input and to discuss more abstract, thought-provoking themes. Community Contact Tasks give students the opportunity to practise their English in real-life situations outside the classroom. Clear illustrations, a lively format, and a wide variety of activities keep students interested and involved.

Canadian Concepts 5 is made up of ten self-contained units. Core activities focus on authentic reading, listening, and video materials. Video clips have been selected from CBC news programs such as *Market Place, Venture,* and *Country Canada.* A wide variety of activity types involve students in productive learning activities. Grammar and writing activities provide ample opportunity for practice and expression.

Throughout the units, students are asked to work on challenging materials that focus on social and cultural issues, and to deal with problems they might encounter in a new country. Each unit concludes with an "In Your Opinion" activity that encourages students to voice their opinions on the theme they have covered. A "Sharpen Your English" feature takes a fun approach to exploring some of the idiosyncrasies of the language.

Teachers and students will appreciate the simple format and lively appearance of the materials, with clear illustrations that lend valuable visual support. They will also enjoy browsing through the Canadian Capsules that provide valuable background information on Canada.

KEY TO SYMBOLS

 Work with a partner

 Discussion activity

 Work in a group

 Video activity

 Writing activity

 Listening activity

 Reading activity

Teacher's Manual and Resource Package

A comprehensive Teacher's Manual and Resource Package provides a wide scope of activities for building academic and professional skills, including skills needed for various types of writing, note-taking, and oral reporting. It also includes an answer key and tape scripts.

At the End of the Course

Students who successfully complete this level will be ready for *Canadian Concepts 6,* a course based on authentic, linguistically challenging newspaper and magazine articles as well as audio and video interviews and passages from CBC programs. They will be ready to participate in debates and controversial discussions and to practise advanced linguistic skills.

UNIT 1

CANADA: WHO ARE THE PEOPLE?

WHO WE ARE

Work in a group and discuss these questions.

1. What is your name?

2. How do you like to be addressed?

3. Where do you come from? (country and city)

4. What language or languages are spoken in your culture?

5. How many languages do you speak?

6. How long have you been here?

7. What parts of Canada have you lived in, or visited?

8. What impressions of Canada would you like to share?

CANADIAN CAPSULES

According to the United Nations Human Development Index, Canada rates second among the top 15 countries in terms of people having the best chance to improve their lives.

1

THE GREAT CANADIAN QUIZ

What do you know about Canada? Do this quiz to find out. Work in a group. Choose the best answers.

1. Where do nine out of ten Canadians live?
   a) in Ontario and Quebec
   b) in western Canada
   c) close to the United States border

2. How many time zones are there in Canada?
   a) three
   b) seven
   c) nine

3. Which vegetable do Canadians eat most?
   a) corn
   b) carrots
   c) potatoes

4. "Bigfoot" is a monster that is said to live in Canada. Its other name is:
   a) the Loch Ness Monster
   b) the Sasquatch
   c) Dracula

5. Which famous cheese was first produced in Ontario?
   a) cheddar
   b) mozzarella
   c) parmesan

6. What information on an address identifies Canada's eighteen geographical regions?
   a) the area code
   b) the postal code
   c) the name of the province

7. Which is the largest island in Canada?
   a) Newfoundland
   b) Baffin Island
   c) Vancouver Island

8. If it is 10:00 a.m. in Ottawa, what time is it in Vancouver?
   a) 5:00 a.m.
   b) 7:00 a.m.
   c) 2:00 p.m.

9. What did Frederick G. Banting discover?
   a) how to fly a plane
   b) how to isolate insulin
   c) how to send radio signals

10. Which fruit does not grow in Canada?
    a) the grape
    b) the peach
    c) the orange

11. Where does "Anne of Green Gables" come from?
    a) New Brunswick
    b) Prince Edward Island
    c) Newfoundland

12. The world's biggest Easter Egg is in:
    a) Vegreville, Alberta
    b) Windsor, Ontario
    c) Kiev, Ukraine

13. What percentage of Canada's total area is farmland?
    a) 7 percent
    b) 27 percent
    c) 47 percent

14. What does CTV stand for?
    a) Canadian Tax Victims
    b) Canadian Television Network
    c) Canadian Transport Vehicles

15. Which is the highest Canadian waterfall?
    a) Takkakaw Falls
    b) Niagara Falls
    c) Angel Falls

16. Which famous apple was first produced in Ontario?
    a) Golden Delicious
    b) McIntosh
    c) Spartan

17. Laura Secord became a famous figure in the War of 1812. Now "Laura Secord" is:
    a) a coffee shop
    b) a chocolate store
    c) a clothing store

18. Which city has the biggest shopping mall?
    a) New York
    b) Edmonton
    c) Toronto

19. If someone in New Brunswick offered you a fiddlehead, what would you do with it?
    a) play music
    b) read it
    c) eat it

20. Which is the largest chartered bank in Canada?
    a) Howard Bank
    b) National Bank of Canada
    c) Royal Bank of Canada

21. Canada's currency is regulated by:
    a) the Royal Canadian Mint
    b) the RCMP
    c) the Bank of Canada

22. Which two famous soft drinks originated in Toronto?
    a) Canada Dry and Orange Crush
    b) Canada Dry and 7-Up
    c) Diet Pepsi and ginger ale

23. The town of Dryden in Northern Ontario has the world's biggest statue of:
    a) a beaver
    b) a moose
    c) a black bear

24. What are "Bow Valley" and "Writing-on-Stone"?
    a) Canadian rock groups
    b) provincial parks in Alberta
    c) grains grown in the prairies

THE AVERAGE CANADIAN

A What do you think is typical of people in Canada? Work in a group and predict whether the following statements are true (**T**) or false (**F**).

The average Canadian adult:

1. woman is 160 cm (5 feet 3 inches) tall

2. man is 175 cm (5 feet 8 inches) tall

3. has a 30 percent chance of remaining single

4. woman marries at 23 years of age

5. man marries at 28 years of age

6. has two children

7. shares housework equally with his or her spouse

8. spends a third of his or her income on housing

9. sleeps 7.5 hours per night

10. drives about 45 minutes to get to work

11.   has a one-in-four chance of being a crime victim

12.   has a high-school education

13.   participates in recycling programs at home or work

14.   lives on a farm or in the country

15.   participates in competitive sports

16.   is confident about his or her economic future

17.   is an immigrant or first-generation Canadian

18.   feels patriotic about Canada

19.   votes in local and federal elections

20.   tries to eat healthy food

B   Read the article to check your answers.

The Average Canadian

ethnic

No one is really an average Canadian, of course. Canada is a vast country with many regional customs and an increasingly diverse ethic population. Nevertheless, there are some generalities that apply to a greater or lesser extent to most of us and most of our neighbours. It is interesting to see the general patterns that make up our society today.

What does the average Canadian adult look like? The people we see on television or in advertisements are probably not typical in height and weight, but taller and thinner than most of us. The average woman weighs 60 kg (132 pounds) and is 160 cm (5 feet 3 inches) tall. The average man weighs 77 kg (170 pounds) and is 170 cm (5 feet 7 inches) tall.

What about lifestyle? Both men and women sleep an average of 8 hours per night. After a typical breakfast of toast or cereal and coffee, they head out for work. They spend about half an hour getting to their places of employment. About a third of their income is spent on housing. After that, food is the biggest expense in the average household.

At the end of the day, Canadian adults come home to their families. The average family has two children, but the burden of caring for them is not shared equally by men and women. It has been estimated that the average woman spends about three hours a day on household tasks and childcare. The average man spends only about an hour a day on the same tasks.

Although one third of Canadians do not marry, the majority of Canadians still choose to marry at some time in their lives. The average age for marriage for a woman today is 25, while men generally marry two years later. About 30 percent of Canadians remain single.

➡

While the average adult Canadian doesn't take part in competitive sports, as he or she may have done when younger, most Canadians attach some importance to the idea of exercising and staying physically fit. They are also inclined to be more concerned about their diets than in the past. People are increasingly avoiding fatty foods, for instance. And organic foods are becoming more popular with many people. On the other hand, although conscious of the harmful effects of cigarettes, many Canadians are still inclined to smoke.

Canadians on average are better educated than they were in the past. One hundred years ago, 50 percent of the population lived on farms and had only three or four years of schooling. Today the average Canadian is a high-school graduate and is more likely to work in a white-collar job in a city than on a farm or in a blue-collar job. Yet there is a high level of uncertainty about the economic future among many members of the workforce and people generally feel pessimistic about their retirement prospects.

Many Canadians feel a sense of civic responsibility. The majority participate in recycling programs either at home or at work. Canadians also feel that government has a responsibility to control pollution. Most Canadians vote in both local and federal elections and follow political issues on radio and television and in the papers. Canadians are proud of their country but most would not describe themselves as patriotic flag-wavers. On the negative side, Canadians today stand a one-in-four chance of being victims of crime within the next year.

With 250 000 newcomers entering Canada every year, immigrants and first-generation Canadians now outnumber Canadians whose families have been here for generations. Whatever their origins, however, Canadians share the same basic concerns: having a decent job, access to education, and raising children in a happy and healthy environment.

WHAT ABOUT YOU?

A   In a group, talk about the quiz.

1.   How many answers did you get correct?

2.   How many answers surprised you?

B   Discuss the ideas in the article.

1.   How close are you to the "average Canadian"?

2.   In what ways are you different?

3.   How do you feel about the interests that most Canadians share: "raising children, having a job and access to education"? Are these your biggest concerns?

4.   Can you think of any other concerns many Canadians share?

WRITE ABOUT YOU

Write about yourself. Compare yourself to the average Canadian in the article. How similar or different is your life? What hopes and concerns do you share with the average Canadian?

Reflexive Pronouns

Reflexive pronouns are used when the subject and object in a sentence refer to the same person.

> **I** wrote a composition about **myself**.
>
> **We** all wrote about **ourselves**.

Reflexive pronouns have the singular ending **self**, or the plural ending **selves**.

> my**self**
> your**self**
> him**self**
> her**self**
> it**self**
>
> our**selves**
> your**selves**
> them**selves**

A   Match the correct form of the reflexive pronouns.

1. immigrants   a) myself
2. my lawyer   b) himself
3. you and your family   c) yourself
4. that lady   d) itself
5. the computer   e) themselves
6. my brother-in-law   f) herself
7. me alone   g) ourselves
8. you alone   h) himself or herself
9. me and my aunt   i) yourselves

B   Use reflexive pronouns to complete the sentences.

1. Why don't you all just help _____ to some coffee?

2. Marie excused _____ and left the classroom quickly.

3. He wasn't bored because he knew how to amuse _____.

4. The cat got up and stretched _____ before walking away.

5. I was alone so I decided to introduce _____ to the woman.

6. The children helped _____ to milk and cookies after school.

7. Let me help you. You can't carry that heavy box _____.

8. The parents chose the name for the child _____.

9. We didn't need help. We found the classroom _____.

10. Don't ask me. You can look up the information _____.

CANADIAN, EH?

Use the verbs below to complete the paragraph.

**to maintain   take on   populated   make up   joining in
born   to assimilate   known**

Both Canada and the United States are countries that are
___1_____ by many people who were ___2_____ in
different countries. The United States is known as a melting pot. This
means that immigrants are expected ___3_____ into American
culture and ___4_____ the values and language of the new
country as quickly as possible. Canada, on the other hand, is
___5_____ as a cultural mosaic. This means that the various
cultural groups that ___6_____ the population are encouraged
___7_____ their own customs and languages while
___8_____ with the society around them.

CANADIAN CAPSULES

In a recent poll of 1800 Canadians, 84 percent of those interviewed said they considered understanding their inner selves more important than money or success.

THE NUMBER OF CANADIANS

  A   Work with a partner. Practise saying these big numbers.

23 341 638   twenty-three million
three hundred and forty-one thousand
six hundred and thirty-eight

26 087 536   twenty-six million
eighty-seven thousand
five hundred and thirty-six

19 203 054   nineteen million
two hundred and three thousand
and fifty-four

  B   Exchange information.

Partner A: Use the information below.

Partner B: Turn to page 15.

Partner A

1.   Your partner has the same text with the numbers missing. Read your text aloud and let your partner fill in the missing numbers.

Until the 1970s, most immigrants to Canada came from Britain. About **26 490** people came from Britain, which was slightly more than the **24 323** people who came from the United States. Large numbers of immigrants came from Portugal (**7902** people), Greece (**6345** people), and India (**5649** people).

In the 1980s, immigrants arrived from many places. Vietnam provided **25 541** people, Britain **18 245** people, and the United States **9926**. Hong Kong was next in line, with **6309** immigrants, slightly ahead of Laos, the source of **5041** immigrants.

2.   Listen to your partner and fill in the missing numbers. Use the worksheet.

In the early 1990s, Hong Kong led the way with _**1**_____ immigrants to Canada. Poland ranked second, with _**2**_____ immigrants, followed by Lebanon with _**3**_____. During this period, _**4**_____ people arrived from the Philippines, and _**5**_____ from India. Vietnam followed with _**6**_____ immigrants. The number of immigrants from Portugal was about _**7**_____; from China _**8**_____; and from the United States _**9**_____. There were _**10**_____ immigrants from El Salvador.

C   Work with your partner. Read the sentences below and write **T** (true) or **F** (false) together. Correct false information.

1.   The biggest source of immigrants to Canada in the 1970s was the United States.

2.   More people immigrated to Canada from Greece than from India during the 1970s.

3.   The leading source of immigrants to Canada in the 1990s was China.

4.   More immigrants came to Canada from Laos than from Hong Kong in the 1980s.

5.   In the 1990s, more people immigrated from Poland than from Lebanon.

6.   More Chinese than Portuguese came to Canada as immigrants in the 1990s.

7.   In the 1980s, the biggest source of immigrants to Canada was Vietnam.

8.   Many more people came to Canada from Britain than from the United States in the 1970s.

9.   More people came to Canada from Vietnam than from Hong Kong in the 1980s.

10. More immigrants came to Canada from Lebanon than from India in the 1990s.

ENTERING CANADA

LISTENING ACTIVITY 1   *Interview with Richard Goldman, Immigration Lawyer*

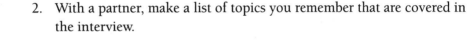

A Work in a group to discuss these questions.

1. List some of the reasons why people emigrate from their home countries.

2. What are some of the reasons why people immigrate to **Canada**?

3. Which parts of Canada do you think attract the most immigrants?

4. What kind of people is Immigration Canada most likely to admit?

5. What are some of the questions immigration officers ask potential immigrants to Canada?

6. What are some good and bad sources of advice about immigration regulations?

B 1. Listen to the interview and decide what the main idea of the interview is:

  a) regulations for different categories of immigrants

  b) what landed immigrants have to do to become citizens

  c) what reasons are valid when applying for refugee status

  d) how long it takes to become a Canadian citizen

2. With a partner, make a list of topics you remember that are covered in the interview.

C Listen for details. To prepare, read the questions with a partner. Then listen and answer the questions. Use the worksheet.

1. Where can a person apply if he or she wants to immigrate to Canada?

2. How long does it take for an application to be processed?

3. How many people is Canada presently accepting?

4. Who has the best chance of being accepted into Canada?

5. What other groups of people have a good chance of acceptance?

6. If someone from another country marries a Canadian, will he or she be accepted into Canada?

7. What is a "permanent resident"?

8. What rights do permanent residents have?

9. Under what conditions can a person lose his or her permanent resident status?

10. What does a landed immigrant have to do to become a Canadian citizen?

11. On what basis would a person be excluded from immigrating to Canada?

12. If a person is born in Canada but lives elsewhere, is he or she a Canadian citizen?

13. Does Canada have a policy of dual citizenship?

14. Under what conditions does Canada accept a refugee?

15. How can a person obtain refugee status?

IN MY OPINION

The Best Place to Live

A What makes a country a good place to live? In a group, put the categories below in order from most important to least important.

education

health care

personal safety

freedom of speech

job opportunities

the environment

transportation

the weather

the cost of living

human rights

community services

life expectancy

family life

the crime rate

religious freedom

B Canada is ranked by the United Nations as one of the best places to live. Do you agree or disagree? Give your opinions about Canada and any other countries you know, using the categories in the list.

C Write about your opinion. Which country is a good place to live? Explain your views.

SHARPEN YOUR ENGLISH

What Do You Say?

Work in groups. Choose the best response in each of the situations.

1. You don't understand what someone has just said.
   a) "Say that again."
   b) "I beg your pardon."
   c) "What did you say?"

2. You want to invite someone to sit down with you.
   a) "Would you like to join me?"
   b) "Sit down over here."
   c) "Why are you standing there?"

3. You want to pass someone in a narrow space.
   a) "Get out of my way please."
   b) "You are in my way. Please move."
   c) "Excuse me please"

4. You are with a group of people and you want to smoke.
   a) "Do you have a cigarette?"
   b) "Does anyone mind if I smoke?"
   c) "Would someone pass the ashtray over here?"

5. You want someone to go through the doorway ahead of you.
   a) "You can go first."
   b) "After you, please."
   c) "It's your turn."

6. Someone near you sneezes.
   a) "Bless you."
   b) "Are you sick?"
   c) "Excuse me."

7. You want to hand something to someone.

   a) "Here you are."

   b) "Take this."

   c) "Hold it."

8. You see that someone is about to walk into something.

   a) "Be careful."

   b) "Look out!"

   c) "Take care."

9. You want to offer someone your seat on the bus.

   a) "Would you like to sit down?"

   b) "Here. Take my seat."

   c) "Take this seat. I don't need to sit."

10. You call your friend Mike on the phone.

    a) "Who is this?"

    b) "Is Mike there please?"

    c) "Where is Mike?"

11. You want to know the time and you don't have a watch on.

    a) "Hey, what time do you have?"

    b) "Tell me what time you have."

    c) "Could you tell me the time, please?"

12. You don't agree with what someone has said.

    a) "I see it a bit differently."

    b) "You are wrong about that."

    c) "That's not true. I disagree."

13. You can't remember someone's name.

    a) I'm sorry, I forgot your name.

    b) Who are you?

    c) What's your name, again?

14. You want to pay for your meal in a restaurant.

    a) "Excuse me, can I have the check please?"

    b) "Server, come here."

    c) "How much is it?"

15. Someone has just pushed into a line in front of you.

    a) "Excuse me. I was already in line here."

    b) "What do you think you are doing anyway?"

    c) "It's not your turn. Go to the back of the line."

16. You accidentally dial the wrong number on the telephone.

    a) "Who is this?"

    b) "I'm sorry. I must have the wrong number."

    c) "Are you sure this isn't the number I called?"

THE NUMBER OF CANADIANS

Partner B

1. Listen to your partner read the text. Fill in the missing numbers. Use the worksheet.

   Until the 1970s, most immigrants to Canada came from Britain. About ___1_____ people came from Britain, which was slightly more than the _2_____ people who came from the United States. Large numbers of immigrants came from Portugal (_3_____ people), Greece (_4_____ people), and India (_5_____ people).

   In the 1980s, immigrants arrived from many places. Vietnam provided ___6_____ people, Britain _7_____ people, and the United States _8_____. Hong Kong was next in line, with _____9_____ immigrants, slightly ahead of Laos, the source of _____10_____ immigrants.

2. Read your text while your partner fills in the missing numbers.

   In the early 1990s, Hong Kong led the way with **28 825** immigrants to Canada. Poland ranked second, with **16 492** immigrants, followed by Lebanon with **12 407**. During this period, **11 950** people arrived from the Philippines, and **10 570** from India. Vietnam followed with **9048** immigrants. The number of immigrants from Portugal was about **7906**; from China **7848**; and from the United States **5906**. There were **3752** immigrants from El Salvador.

CANADIAN CAPSULES

The population of Canada is growing at a faster rate than that of any other western industrial nation.

2

WHAT'S THERE TO EAT?

OUR EATING HABITS

A First, read the paragraph. Then complete it with any words that are logical.

North Americans have some _____ eating habits. Not only do _____ eat three meals a day, but _____ also eat several snacks a day. _____ eat in their cars, and _____ eat lots of fast food. _____ they don't have time to _____, they pick up _____ on the way home from _____ or school. We may think _____ this is new, but snacking _____ been a way of _____ for a long time.

17

B With a partner, read the following sentences and discuss whether they are true or false.

1. Popcorn was invented 50 years ago in America.

2. Bananas originally came from Central America.

3. The pretzel is shaped to look like a person praying.

4. Sandwiches were created for a lazy gambler.

5. Chocolate bars were invented in the 1920s.

6. Early people ate wild berries, roots, and fruit as snacks.

7. The first candy was made by the Egyptians 3000 years ago.

8. Bagels were created in Montreal 35 years ago.

9. The potato chip was created when a customer complained that his fried potatoes were too thick.

10. Peanuts, as snacks, became popular at the circus.

11. The Oreo cookie is the best selling cooking in the world.

12. The first sugar-free soft drink was Diet Coke.

13. Soft, frozen yogurt was invented at the same time as soft ice cream.

C Look at the time line at the bottom of pages 18–21 to check your answers.

D Find out about the eating habits of students in the class. Talk with three other students, and complete the chart on page 19. Use the worksheet.

Time Line

People in Mexico ate popcorn similar to the type we have today.

The banana, an herb, was discovered in the Indus Valley of present day Pakistan.

| 400 000 BC | 3000 BC | 1000 BC | 327 BC |

Homo erectus, early human, looked for berries, roots, wild grains, fruit, and vegetables as snacks.

The first candy was invented in Egypt. It was made of seeds, nuts, dried fruit, and spices, held together with honey.

How often do you do the following?	Student A	Student B	Student C
1. cook a meal of several courses			
2. order in supper			
3. go out for brunch			
4. eat dinner with family or friends			
5. eat alone			
6. invite people to your home for dinner			
7. eat dinner in a restaurant			
8. pick up ready-made food on your way home			
9. eat a frozen dinner			
10. try new foods in a restaurant			
11. experiment with cooking a new food			
12. bring your lunch to work or class			
13. eat lunch in a fast-food restaurant			
14. eat a good breakfast			
15. skip breakfast			

THE 7-MINUTE MEAL

A Scan the article for the answers to these questions:

1. How did people prepare food in the past?
2. What is different about the way people prepare meals today?
3. What is new in supermarkets today?

Bagels were created in
Krakow, Poland.

610 — **1610** — **1762**

The pretzel was created
by a monk, in the
shape of arms folded
in prayer.

Potato chips were invented
by an angry chef in
Saratoga Springs, when a
customer complained that his
fried potatoes were too
thick.

The 7-Minute Meal

Judy Schultz

Nobody would ever argue against the joys of eating a home-cooked meal. The problem arises when there's nobody home to cook it. And that, in the '90s, is increasingly the case. One American futurist suggests that by 2000, the average time spent preparing meals will be seven minutes a day. Talk about fast food.

According to Bryan Walton of the Canadian Council of Grocery Distributors, home-meal replacement is one of the biggest trends in retail food sales today. Added-value meals—prepared or semi-prepared—have taken the time factor out of getting a home-cooked meal on the table. Meals that were once planned a week in advance are now planned during the 30-minute commute from office to home, with a stop en route at the local supermarket. The microwave oven has eased the cook's departure from the stove.

Recent studies of consumer shopping habits in Canada suggest that two-thirds of Canadians are now resorting to taking meals home that have been prepared outside their homes in such places as a deli or a pizza parlour. (About one-fifth of shoppers take home prepared meals from the supermarket.)

Walton points out that just 20 years ago, a stroll down the average produce aisle would have turned up around 60 items. Today, it's closer to 300. And tucked in among the fennel and the enoki mushrooms are a host of items known as "added value."

Chunks of melon and six perfect strawberries packaged with a dip. Carrot sticks. Bags of shredded broccoli stems, ready for salad or a stir-fry. Cut-up and pre-mixed Chinese vegetables, ready for the wok.

Time, and convenience, are the added values for which today's shopper is willing to pay. If you whip over to the meat counter, you'll find speedy versions of chicken, beef and pork, either cut in such small pieces that they'll stir-fry in minutes (some with vegetables and seasoning packs included) or marinated, pre-seasoned and arranged on skewers for the barbecue. Even the lowly meatball is available fresh and pre-formed, frozen and uncooked, frozen and cooked, or frozen, cooked and sauced.

If all of this sounds like bad news for the dedicated food lover, it's not. The variety of foods stocked in supermarkets has mushroomed. Shelf after shelf of specialty vinegars, a dozen varieties of lettuce, fresh herbs, imported cheese, and fresh pasta are everyday fare.

A bewildering variety of spices, sauces and marinades confronts the eager cook, with everything from fresh coriander to tamari sauce to garam masala. In part, this is attributed to the strong ethnic influence both from our

The sandwich was born when John Montagu, the Earl of Sandwich, refused to leave the table when gambling, and ordered sliced meat and cheese served to him between slices of bread.

1853

1880s

Peanuts became popular as snacks when P.T. Barnum began marketing them in nickel-sized bags at his circus.

Animal Crackers were packaged in boxes that were designed as Christmas tree ornaments.

1902

immigrant populations and from well-travelled cooks. Not only do we want to eat couscous in Morocco, but we want to cook it when we're back home, and have it ready in less than 10 minutes.

In-store demonstrations have become an important tool in introducing shoppers to new flavours and products. On the average Saturday (the heaviest shopping day), it's possible to snack your way through a supermarket.

In the bakery department, variety is all. As well as all the old standbys and the specialty products, such as edible sourdough bread bowls, there's a strong move toward the old-style loaves our great-great-grandmothers baked on their home turf, back in Europe, Asia or the Middle East. Foccacia, bruschetta, heavy rye, pita, crostini, tortillas, chapati. Even the Chinese specialty green onion cake is available frozen.

 B Read the article again and answer the questions below.

1.   Why is it harder to get a home-cooked meal in the '90s than in the past?

2.   Where does the planning of meals often take place today?

3.   What is true of two-thirds of meals Canadians consume today?

4.   What are some examples of "added value" items at the supermarket?

5.   What are two things for which shoppers are willing to pay extra?

6.   Give an example of how the variety of foods stocked has "mushroomed."

7.   Which two factors have resulted in a strong ethnic influence in the products available in supermarkets today?

8.   What role do "in-store demonstrations" play?

9.   What is meant by the "old standbys" in the last paragraph?

10. What is meant by the phrase "on their home turf" in the last paragraph?

Chocolate bars, such as Baby Ruth and Oh Henry! were invented.

Royal Crown Cola introduced Diet-Rite Cola, the first sugar-free soft drink.

1912   **1920**   **1962**   **1972**

The Oreo cookie became the top-selling cookie in the world, with more than five billion eaten in North American annually.

Soft frozen yogurt was invented in Boston by putting yogurt through an ice cream machine.

 **Present Perfect for Indefinite Past Time**

Use the present perfect when the time that an action took place **is not known** or **is not important**.

> I **have been** to New York many times.

The use of this verb form invites general questions:

> Do you like it there?
> What's it like?

Use the simple past when an action **was completed in past time**.

> I **visited** New York.

The use of the simple past tense invites time-related questions:

> When did you go? Did you have a good time?
> Did you see the Empire State Building?

To form the present perfect, use the auxiliary verb **have** and the past participle of the main verb.

> I **have** often **eaten** oysters.

 Check your knowledge of verb forms by completing this chart.

Present	Past	Past participle
(be) am/is/are		been
	became	become
begin	began	
blow	blew	
break		broken
	brought	brought
buy	bought	
catch		caught
come	came	
choose		chosen
cost	cost	
cut		cut
do		done
draw	drew	
drink		drunk

➡

drive	drove	
eat		eaten
feel	felt	
	found	found
forget		forgotten
get	got	
give	gave	
	went	gone
have		had
hear	heard	
hold		held
keep	kept	
	knew	known
lose		lost
make	made	
meet		met
	paid	paid
put		put
read	read	
ride		ridden
ring	rang	
run	ran	
see		seen
sell	sold	
send		sent
shake	shook	
show	showed	
sing		sung
sit		sat
sleep		slept
speak	spoke	
	stood	stood
swim	swam	
take		taken
teach	taught	
tell		told
think	thought	
understand		understood
wear		worn
win	won	
write	wrote	

B   Choose the correct verb and put it in the present perfect form.

drink be eat become teach know see begin taste give

1.   Jenna isn't hungry. She _____ already.

2.   My uncle _____ three cups of tea today.

3.   My grandmother _____ many people how to cook.

4.   Max and Nina _____ to speak English really well.

5.   Ben and I _____ to that restaurant several times.

6.   Carolyn _____ many parties like this one.

7.   Jun and Min Hee _____ each other for years.

8.   They _____ strange foods in many different countries.

9.   Michiko _____ an expert in cooking Italian food.

10. The traveller _____ how people eat in other lands.

C   Choose the simple past or the present perfect form of the verb.

1.   Marco (wore/has worn) his new jacket to the party last night.

2.   Jun and Lily (ate/have eaten) at my house many times.

3.   Suzanne (tried/has tried) every French restaurant in town.

4.   David (learned/has learned) to prepare sushi in Japan.

5.   My uncle (worked/has worked) in a café when he was young.

6.   The microwave oven (made/has made) cooking much faster.

7.   They (found/have found) the pizzeria by asking directions.

8.   The cook (used/has used) the same recipe for many years.

9.   Junko (forgot/has forgotten) how to make sushi since she came to Canada.

10. Terry (acquired/has acquired) a taste for snails in France.

11. Last night's dinner party (took/has taken) a lot of planning.

12. Jane and Tim (thought/have thought) of everything yesterday.

13. The server (brought/has brought) our coffee right after dinner.

14. Max (lost/has lost) the name of the restaurant on the way to meet us.

15. Many of the guests (were/have been) here for dinner before.

INTERNATIONAL DINING

What do you know about food customs in other cultures? Work in groups to discuss these questions. Choose the best answers.

1. Where do people eat with a fork in the left hand and a knife in the right hand?

    a) European countries

    b) North America

    c) Asian countries

2. In China, which of these is **not** a good gift for a hostess?

    a) a fan

    b) a clock

    c) flowers

3. In which country is punctuality very important?

    a) Indonesia

    b) Venezuela

    c) Sweden

4. Which of these is considered bad luck in many European countries?

    a) an uneven number of flowers

    b) an unwrapped bouquet

    c) an even number of flowers

5. To get a server's attention in a restaurant in Canada:

    a) snap your fingers

    b) try to catch the server's eye

    c) call out, "Waiter!"

6. If you visit someone's house in Canada, you should:

    a) leave right after the meal

    b) stay until the hosts start yawning

    c) stay and chat for a while

7. Where do people generally eat fruit with a knife and fork?

    a) Japan

    b) France

    c) Malaysia

8. What is the proper way to place chopsticks when you are not eating with them?

    a)   straight up in a bowl of rice

    b)   on either side of the plate

    c)   together, on one side of the plate

9. In which language is "salud" a toast?

    a)   German

    b)   Russian

    c)   Spanish

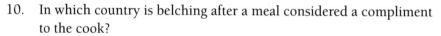

10. In which country is belching after a meal considered a compliment to the cook?

    a)   Taiwan

    b)   Turkey

    c)   Mexico

11. Which people believe you should accept food only after it is offered three times?

    a)   Americans

    b)   the British

    c)   Koreans

12. People from Asia rarely put these on the table:

    a)   napkins

    b)   knives

    c)   fruit

13. In Japan, finishing all the rice in your bowl means:

    a)   you would like more

    b)   you have finished the meal

    c)   you would like to eat something different

14. Many people believe that chicken soup will:

    a)   cure a cold

    b)   make you strong

    c)   cure a toothache

15. People in Vietnam traditionally celebrate their birthdays:

    a)   on the date they were born

    b)   at the beginning of the month they were born

    c)   on New Year's Day

16. In Spain, people generally eat dinner:
    a) at noon
    b) at 7 p.m.
    c) at 10 p.m.

17. In Italy and France, salads are often served:
    a) before the meal
    b) with the meal
    c) after the meal

18. Sushi, or raw fish, is a favourite dish in:
    a) China
    b) Indonesia
    c) Japan

19. Which popular North American food do most cultures consider animal food?
    a) sweet potatoes
    b) onions
    c) corn on the cob

20. In Germany and Switzerland, it is considered rude to:
    a) put your elbows on the table
    b) put your hands in your lap
    c) put your napkin in your lap

EXPERIENCES IN DINING

 LISTENING ACTIVITY 2 *Interview with Marian Thompson, Food Writer*

  A Read and discuss the anecdote below. What did Ronya misunderstand?

Ronya, a young woman from Sweden, was travelling through the United States and Canada. She came to stay with a family in Vancouver for a few months, to perfect her English. When Ronya was unpacking her bags, her hostess noticed that she had a large collection of forks, and that no two forks were alike. She asked her about this unusual collection. Ronya explained, "Whenever I eat at someone's house in America, the hostess always tells me, as she clears the table: 'Keep your fork.' So I do."

B   Listen for the main idea of the passage:

a)   food customs in Asia

b)   the role of the host and hostess

c)   misunderstandings at the table

d)   favourite foods in other countries

 C   Read the questions with a partner. Then, listen and answer. Use the worksheet.

1.   Why did Carol invite Ricardo's relatives to her home?

2.   Why did she serve the food "buffet-style"?

3.   How had Carol offended her guests?

4.   What did Mark do when he sat down with the other guests?

5.   Why did the hostess refill his bowl?

6.   What happened every time he emptied his bowl?

7.   What did emptying a bowl mean in his girlfriend's culture?

8.   Why do Egyptians and Filipinos leave a little food on the plate?

9.   What does leaving food on your plate mean in Indonesia?

10.   What does cleaning your plate mean in Japan?

11.   How can you find out what to do when you eat dinner with people of a different culture?

12.   Why is it a good idea to find out about your host's customs beforehand?

HOW DO YOU EAT IT?

   Here is a list of foods from different parts of the world. Work in a group and discuss **in detail** how you would eat these foods. Get suggestions from different people in the group.

1.   couscous

2.   a mango

3.   an apple

4.   pizza

5.   kiwi

6.   oysters

7.   café au lait

8.   a hamburger

9.   crab

10.   spaghetti

11.   soup

12.   shish kebab

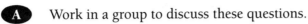

THE PIZZA POLICE

 CBC

VIDEO ACTIVITY 1

A Work in a group to discuss these questions.

1. How often do you eat pizza?

2. What different sizes of pizza can you order?

3. What toppings do you think are most popular?

4. What is your favourite kind of pizza?

5. How do you prefer to eat pizza—with your hands or with a fork?

B Watch the video and answer these questions. Use the worksheet.

1. What are some toppings Canadians like to put on pizza?

2. Where is the International Pizza Association based?

3. What aspects of making pizza do the rules touch on?

4. According to Giovanna, how should pizza dough be made?

5. How should pizza be baked?

6. What size is the ideal pizza?

7. Name some toppings Giovanna doesn't approve of.

8. What does she say about putting pineapple on pizza?

9. How is real Neapolitan pizza made?

C Choose the correct words to complete the story.

If the Italians had their (**1.** customs, ideas, way) there would be no more Domino's Pizza or Pizza Hut. They (**2.** eat, say, make) this type of pizza is not the real thing, and have come up with a set of rules to (**3.** follow, cook, invent) to make true, or authentic, pizza from Naples.

To Italians, good pizza (**4.** eats, starts, sells) with a good crust. It must be mixed, shaped, and (**5.** washed, baked, fried) fresh in a wood-burning oven at 800 degrees. Only a few (**6.** recipes, vegetables, toppings), such as fresh chopped tomatoes, olive oil and garlic, should be added. And the pizza (**7.** does, must, have) be plate-sized, not hanging over the edge of the (**8.** table, plate, counter).

The guardians of traditional Italian pizza want people to stop making the kind of pizza Americans love—lots of extra cheese, with assorted toppings (**9.** like, such, soon) as pepperoni, mushrooms, and green pepper. They are

➡

horrified at some of the (**10.** new, old, traditional) toppings that have been added: fresh pineapple, strawberries, or kiwi—even lotus root, which was seen on pizza in Japan.

Still, they understand that pizza has become big (**11.** food, business, snacks) and that compromises have to be made. One Neapolitan pizza maker even allows caviar and smoked salmon on his pizza. (**12.** And, For, But) he sticks to tradition when it comes to eating the pizza. "It's better not to use a knife and fork. You have to eat it with your (**13.** dish, spoon, hands)", he says.

IN MY OPINION

An Apple a Day

Look at the proverbs below. Work in a group. First, decide what the proverbs mean. Then discuss which ones you agree or disagree with.

1. An apple a day keeps the doctor away.

2. One man's meat is another man's poison.

3. Too many cooks spoil the broth.

4. Bread is the staff of life.

5. If you want your dinner, don't offend the cook.

6. Fish, to be tasty, must swim three times—in water, in butter, and in wine. (Polish proverb)

7. Eat to live; don't live to eat.

8. He that eats least, eats most.

9. Don't bite the hand that feeds you.

10. You can't have your cake and eat it too.

11. Life is like a bowl of cherries.

12. A watched pot never boils.

CANADIAN CAPSULES

The average time spent in a grocery store in Canada is 45 minutes, and the average cost for one visit is about $85.

SHARPEN YOUR ENGLISH

Vocabulary

  A Match the quantitative terms with the foods. Use each food only once.

a head of lettuce

1. a loaf of a) tea
2. a clove of b) celery
3. a bunch of c) cheese
4. a pinch of d) corn
5. a slice of e) salt
6. a pot of f) bananas
7. a leg of g) garlic
8. a stalk of h) bread
9. a pat of i) ice cream
10. a scoop of j) spaghetti
11. a strand of k) lamb
12. an ear of l) butter

B Use the words below to complete the dialogue.

**salt shaker   pits   corkscrew   ice cubes   nutcrackers
tea spoons   oyster shells   swizzle sticks   nut shells
candlesticks   sugar bowl**

Nick and Julie are getting ready to entertain their friends. They plan to serve drinks and light snacks in the living room and then invite their friends to the table for dinner.

Nick: I put the olives on the coffee table, but I forgot a dish for the olive ___1___. Do you think we need ___2___ to stir the drinks?

Julie: Not really. The important thing is to have some ___3___ to cool the drinks. And don't forget a dish near the nuts for the ___4___. Oh yes, maybe we should put out the ___5___, too. Otherwise people won't be able to eat the nuts.

Nick: What about the dinner table? Is there anything missing there? We have cutlery and glasses. And I put the candles in the ___6___.

Julie: Oh, we forgot the __7_____. People might want to season their food. And we need the __8_____ to open the wine.

Nick: We're serving seafood. I guess we need a plate for the __9_____ too. What are we having for dessert again?

Julie: Cake and ice cream. I'm glad you reminded me. We need __10_____ for the ice cream, and we should put out the __11_____ for when we serve the coffee and tea.

Nick: Oh there's the doorbell. That must be our guests.

3

WHAT'S HOT? WHAT'S NOT?

WHAT'S IN STYLE?

Discuss these questions in a group.

1. How often do you shop for new clothes?

2. How often do you buy something that is the latest style?

3. When a style changes, do you buy clothing in the new fashion immediately, after a while, or not at all?

4. Which fashion trends have you followed in the last year or two?

5. Do you think styles change too often or not? Explain your answer.

6. Who do you think is more conscious of style, men or women?

7. If your friend was wearing the latest style, and you thought he or she looked very strange, would you say something?

8. Do you think it is possible to go too far in the name of fashion? (For example, wearing very pointed shoes than can injure your feet.)

FASHION FIRSTS

A Work with a partner to see what you know about fashion through the ages. Decide together whether the statements below are true or false.

1. In ancient Egypt, skirts were worn by men.

2. Blue jeans were invented and became popular about 50 years ago.

3. The idea of having pockets in pants is a recent invention.

4. Before buttons existed, safety pins were used to fasten clothes.

5. Both men and women wore bell-bottom jeans during the 1970s.

6. The first modern running shoe was produced by the Adidas company.

7. Nylon was first invented approximately 25 years ago.

8. Velcro was invented soon after the zipper became popular.

9. In the 1920s, men commonly wore top hats and coats with tails.

10. Women started wearing pants 100 years ago.

11. Calvin Klein was the first designer to market designer jeans.

12. Women began wearing mini skirts during the 1960s.

13. Shoulder pads were popular at the same time as mini-skirts.

14. Men wore their hair longer in the 1950s than in the 1960s.

15. Tight exercise clothes were a popular fashion item in the 1940s.

B Now consult the time line at the bottom of the pages 34–39 to check your answers.

Time Line

Assyrian men had long curled hair and beards.

Buttons were first used in Europe.

| 2300 BC | 800 BC | 200 AD | 1200 | 1580 |

Skirts were a common type of clothing worn by Egyptian men. They often wore one skirt over another.

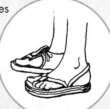

Romans made different shoes for left and right feet.

Pockets were first sewn into men's pants.

WOULD YOU SHAVE YOUR HEAD?

A Work with a partner to complete the paragraphs.

Fashion is always (**1.** old, new, changing). One year women wear short skirts and high (**2.** shoes, heels, pants) and men have long hair. The next year women wear long skirts and flat shoes, and men have (**3.** short, shaved, wide) heads and earrings. People have dyed their (**4.** hair, eyebrows, skin) every colour of the rainbow, and have cut, curled, and straightened it into every (**5.** colour, style, type) imaginable.

Men and women have also painted and decorated every part of their (**6.** bodies, noses, feet) from their earlobes to their toes. They have worn (**7.** sandals, shoes, socks) that are high, low, pointy, or wide and (**8.** belts, shoes, clothes) that show off different body parts, while concealing others. How long has this been going on, and where did (**9.** humankind, fashion, clothes) begin anyway? The answers are probably (**10.** "Soon," "Forever," "Never") and fashion is likely as old as humankind.

CANADIAN CAPSULES

A Canadian company, Dominion Textiles, is the world's largest producer of denim.

Men and women wore fancy, high-heeled shoes trimmed with bows.

Women wore tight-waisted dresses with big skirts.

1600s **1600s–1700s** **1830s** **1849**

Men wore huge, curled wigs.

The safety pin was invented in the United States.

B Work in a group. Discuss who in your group has done, or who would do, each of the following. (Some questions apply to only men or only women.)

1. dye your hair an unusual colour

2. wear very high-heeled shoes

3. get a permanent tattoo

4. cut your hair very short or shave your head

5. wear a torn shirt or torn jeans

6. loose weight or gain weight to be in style

7. get a nose ring

8. grow a beard, moustache, or long sideburns

9. wear unisex cologne

10. wear very tight clothes

11. wear uncomfortable (such as very pointy) shoes

12. grow your hair very long

13. dress completely in black

14. wear fluorescent-coloured clothes

15. refuse to wash as a sign of protest

16. dress like someone of the opposite sex

17. wear see-through clothes

18. wear unusual-coloured lipstick or nail polish

19. wear large shoulder pads

20. get a suntan

Men wore
coats with
tails, and
top hats.

The zipper
was invented
in America.

1800s   **1873**   **1893**   **1917**

Levi Strauss
invented blue
jeans.

The Keds company
produced the first
tennis shoes.

IN THE NAME OF BEAUTY

LISTENING ACTIVITY **3**   *Interview with Judith Markham, Psychologist*

 Read the questions with a partner. Then listen to the interview and answer the questions. Use the worksheet.

1. What have studies shown about people who are especially attractive?

2. How are the heroes and heroines in fairy tales usually described?

3. How did being attractive help women throughout the ages?

4. What are three things people have done to their bodies to look attractive?

5. What body shape is considered attractive in North America?

6. Why are fat people considered beautiful in many countries?

7. What beauty practice changed once people realized how dangerous it was?

8. Why did women eat Arsenic Complexion Wafers in the eighteenth century?

9. Why did women eat a poisonous plant called belladonna?

10. What other product did women use that was dangerous?

11. Why do many people today have plastic surgery?

12. What have people done to enhance their looks throughout the ages?

13. What did archaeologists find evidence of, from 4000 BC?

14. What three things did Roman soldiers do before they went to war?

15. What two things are men doing now to look attractive?

The first synthetic fabrics were produced.

1920s   **1920s**   **1930s**   **1940s**

Women wore the "boyish" look—straight, unfitted dresses that hung to the knee.

Women began to wear pants for playing sports.

Women wore pants outfits with padded shoulders.

 **GRAMMAR FOCUS**   **"Used to," "Still," "Anymore"**

Use the expression **used to** + the base form of the main verb to contrast past habits with present activities.

> She **used to live** with her parents. (Now she lives on her own.)

Use **still** + the present tense when past habits have not changed and continue in the present. Use the negative form of the present tense + **anymore** when past habits do not continue in the present.

> Anne **still lives** with her parents.
> Patty **doesn't live** with her parents **anymore**.

A   Complete a chart similar to the one below. First list any activities from the list that you have done in the past. Then put a check mark (✔) if you still do the activity and an ✘ if you don't do it anymore. Add five activities of your own to the list.

Past activity	Today	Past Activity	Today
wear blue jeans		play a team sport	
fight with my sister or brother		exercise everyday	
travel to work by bus		wear a hat outside	
wear mini skirts (women)		follow fashion trends	
wear a tie to work (men)		spend a lot on clothes	
smoke cigarettes		have a beard (men)	
stay up until 3:00 in the morning		wear bell-bottom pants	
live in the country		have pierced ears	
take music lessons		wear nail polish (women)	
walk to school		live in an apartment	

Men had crew cuts—very short hair that was brushed upwards.

Men grew long hair, beards, and moustaches.

Men and women wore bell-bottom jeans and shirts in bright colours.

1950s   **1957**   **1960s–1970s**   **1960s**   **1970s**

Velcro was patented in Switzerland.

Women wore mini skirts.

B   Discuss your list with a partner and practise using the expressions **used to**, **still**, **anymore** orally.

C   Fill in the blanks with **used to**, **still**, or **anymore**.

1. Karen _____ shop at that store, but now it is too expensive.

2. She always wore her hair long when she was young, and she _____ does.

3. Johnny used to wear bell-bottoms in the 1970s, but he doesn't _____.

4. Yoko knows that smoking is dangerous, but she _____ smokes a little.

5. Some things we _____ wear make us laugh when we think about them now.

6. Jun _____ play tennis regularly, but he doesn't have time to practise anymore.

7. Blue jeans were popular in the 1960s and they are _____ popular today.

8. Marco smoked cigarettes for years, but he doesn't smoke them _____.

9. Mr. Richards _____ live in New York, but now he lives in Toronto.

10. Erin Clark always used to be well-dressed and she _____ dresses well.

Women wore tight-fitting exercise clothes or baggy oversized clothes.

1975

Calvin Klein began the designer jeans era.

1980s

1980s–1990s

Punk clothes included torn, ripped clothing, safety pins, Mohawk hairstyles.

WHO ARE THEY FOOLING?

A Skim the article and answer these questions with a partner.

1. Who is Stella Tennant?
2. Why did people gasp when they saw her on the runway?
3. How does she compare with the average Canadian woman?

Who Are They Fooling?

Lisa Tant

I have seen the face of future fashion and it's so far removed from reality that it's scary. Stella Tennant, the British beanpole, has been signed to an exclusive six-month contract as "the face" of Chanel's fall fashion.

International designer Karl Lagerfeld said he chose Tennant, 22, to represent Chanel because she's different. "She does not have the physical, slightly aggressive glamour that was so popular in the early 1990s." She's different, allright. I'll never forget the gasps that rose from the normally shock-resistant fashion crowd at last October's Chanel show in Paris when Tennant sauntered down the runway in a string bikini. With her black hair, white skin and exposed ribs, she looked like a skeleton heading to a ghostly beach party.

But Tennant's emaciated form couldn't be more different from what's really happening with fashion and women's bodies. According to *People* magazine, the average height and weight of a North American woman are 5-foot-4 (162 cm) and 142 pounds (64.5 kg). The average height and weight of a model are 5-foot-9 (175 cm) and 110 pounds (50 kg).

Vancouver model agent Brenda Wong says that's the standard for Canadian models as well. "High-end fashion clients demand that, but they don't want a model who looks gaunt or sick, with bones protruding. The most popular local models have that glamorous classic and sexy look. They need to have curves for that."

So why are some designers and magazines promoting this thinner-than-thin scarecrow look? Like hipsters and platforms, it's just another recycled trend with a short shelf life. Photographer Neal Barr remembers '60s models being "totally emaciated, veins sticking out, faces literally stencilled in." In the same paragraph, Wilhelmina, a '60s supermodel and agency owner, recalls that she "ate twice a week. In between, it was cigarettes and black coffee."

The reality is that the average person measures nothing close to model standards. And some say that garment sizes have actually increased to accommodate our growing body sizes. "A Size 8 today is larger than the Size 8 of 15 years ago," says Ramsdale. "In general, I'd say it's the equivalent of one size larger. Our measurement specifications have increased by one inch (2.5 cm) over all over the past 10 years."

"Sizing has definitely changed in the past 10 years." Agrees Marsha Ross, editor of Style, the Canadian fashion-trade newspaper. "…The population is getting taller. Larger European and German sizing reflects that. Manufacturers are adjusting their sizes so we don't all end up wearing a Size 90."

In March 1991, *Canadian Marketing Magazine* said baby boomers, on average, gain one pound (.45 kg) a year over the age of 25, and that sizes over 14 represent about 35 percent of the annual clothing market. Size 2, worn by some of Hollywood's hottest bodies, isn't even recorded.

In 1988, the Fashion Group Inc., a New York-based association, published a Special Sizes Report and noted that 38 percent of North American women are smaller than a Size 12. Only about a quarter of North American women fit the profile of the so-called contemporary customer, under Size 14 and over 5 foot 4 (162 cm). Yet approximately 95 percent of fashions are directed to that woman. "We sell the bulk of our goods in a Size 12," says Ramsdale, adding that as the boomers get older, they are wearing their clothing looser and with a more comfortable fit.

If fashion designers and magazines continue to promote standards so far from reality, they may end up losing that precious customer, the boomer who can actually afford high-priced designer fashions.

 B Read the article again and find these details:

1. three words to describe Stella Tennant's body shape.
2. the height and weight of the average North American woman
3. the average height and weight of a model
4. two words to describe local models
5. information about Wilhelmina's eating habits
6. how much measurements have increased over the past 10 years
7. how much weight the average baby boomer gains each year
8. how much of the population is smaller than size 12
9. the profile of the contemporary customer
10. the percentage of fashion directed at the contemporary customer
11. the size of the majority of people
12. the way people wear their clothes as they age

 C Put the words from the article into one of the categories. Write **A** for **appearance**, or **P** for **personality**.

1. gangly	9. petite	17. cheerful
2. pleasant	10. charming	18. aggressive
3. emaciated	11. sweet	19. beanpole
4. chubby	12. cute	20. outgoing
5. gaunt	13. willowy	21. skeleton
6. enthusiastic	14. agreeable	22. attractive
7. plain	15. homely	
8. glamorous	16. nervous	

IN MY OPINION

Does Appearance Count?

Work in a group. Discuss the questions.

1. Do you think it is possible to tell things about people from the way they are dressed?

2. How do you think our physical appearance affects our daily lives?

3. Do you think it is realistic for people to try to look like the models in magazines?

4. How would you rank the following, from most important to least important?
    a) wealth
    b) intelligence
    c) physical appearance
    d) character
    e) personality

5. If you could change your appearance to that of any famous person, who would you choose to look like? Explain why.

Up for Debate

 Choose one of the following topics and prepare to debate.

1. It is reasonable to deny jobs to people on the basis of their appearance if they will be working with the public.

2. Appearance is important for a woman but not for a man.

3. Cosmetic surgery should be included in medical insurance, because being attractive is important for a person's career.

4. Images of fashion models in magazines cause young women to have unrealistic expectations about themselves and are to blame for problems such as anorexia.

  Choose one of the topics and write about it. Be sure to explain and defend your point of view.

A Warning

A beautiful actress once suggested to the writer George Bernard Shaw that they should marry and start a family together. "With my looks and your brains, just think what wonderful children they would be," she said. Shaw replied, "But madam, what if they had **my** looks and **your** brains?"

SHARPEN YOUR ENGLISH

"A" or "An"

To know the correct form of the indefinite article (**a** or **an**) in English you need to know how the word is pronounced. Be careful with the letters **h**, **o**, and **u**.

Before a consonant or **consonant sound**, use **a**.

Consonants:	a teacher, a yak
Consonant sounds:	a uniform, a unicycle

Before a vowel or a **vowel sound**, use **an**.

Vowels:	an apple, an orchestra
Vowel sounds:	an hour, an honest man

 Write **a** or **an** before the following words.

1. item
2. actress
3. university
4. owner
5. unique idea
6. hourly wage
7. pair
8. end
9. original
10. advertisement
11. umbrella
12. one-dollar bill
13. union
14. hurry
15. factory
16. Italian
17. honour
18. unit price
19. unusual way
20. older car

UNIT 4

THE ANIMALS WE LIVE WITH

What do you know about animals? Work in a group and decide on the answers to the questions.

1. Which animal does not live in the Arctic?

    a) the owl

    b) the penguin

    c) the whale

2. Which animal is the number one pet in North America today?

    a) the goldfish

    b) the dog

    c) the cat

3. Which animal has the reputation of being stubborn?

    a) the cat

    b) the donkey

    c) the turtle

4. Which of these animals does not give milk?

    a) the reindeer

    b) the lamb

    c) the cow

5. Which animal is a traditional Thanksgiving food?

    a) the turkey

    b) the goose

    c) the rabbit

6. Which animal is the ancestor of the dog?

    a) the fox

    b) the wolf

    c) the bear

7. Which of these animals is a loner?

    a) the wolf

    b) the cat

    c) the bear

8. What are male bees called?

    a) kings

    b) drones

    c) cells

9. People spend more on food for this animal than for babies.

    a) the dog

    b) the cat

    c) tropical fish

10. Which animal has been on earth ten times longer than humans?

    a) the horse

    b) the pig

    c) the camel

11. Eider down, used to make soft warm quilts, comes from:

    a) ducks

    b) geese

    c) chickens

12. Which fabric comes from a domesticated insect?

    a) cotton

    b) linen

    c) silk

13. If all the babies from **one pair** of rabbits lived, how many would there be in three years?

    a) 77 rabbits

    b) 2000 rabbits

    c) 33 million rabbits

14. Which animal is called our "best friend"?

 a) the horse

 b) the dog

 c) the cow

15. Which animals are sold the most from pet shops?

 a) birds

 b) dogs

 c) goldfish

16. The camel knows when it is near water by:

 a) sight

 b) smell

 c) sound

17. A spider can hear through its ears and:

 a) stomach

 b) feet

 c) antennae

18. Cashmere is a soft kind of wool that comes from a:

 a) lamb

 b) goat

 c) sheep

19. When the polar bear wants to disappear in the snow, it covers:

 a) its paws

 b) its nose

 c) its eyes

20. Which bird cannot fly?

 a) the ostrich

 b) the dove

 c) the pigeon

CANADIAN CAPSULES

"We give them the love we can spare, the time we can spare. In return, dogs have given us their absolute all. It is without a doubt the best deal man has ever made."

Roger Caras, *A Celebration of Dogs* (Times Books)

A   Discuss these questions in a group.

1. List some animals you would expect to see outdoors in a city in Canada.

2. List some animals you would expect to see in a national park in Canada.

3. Which of these animals would you pet or feed in a zoo, park, or campground?

   a) a squirrel   d) a dolphin

   b) a deer   e) a small bear

   c) a rabbit   f) an alligator

4. List some differences between a pet and a wild animal.

5. Do you think that wild animals can become our "friends"? Why or why not?

B   Read the article and answer the questions that follow.

Wildlife Encounters

Joanne Diamond

1. Campers in the Pocono Mountains of eastern Pennsylvania spread peanut butter on the windowsills of their trailers to attract bears. Nearby, a forest ranger arrives to find a family hosing a bear down, while the bear lies on its back, feet in the air. Tourists in southern Florida sign up for tours to pet the dolphins, and even jump in the water to swim with them. Alligators in Florida swim through a canal and end up in a suburban parking lot. A moose falls into the swimming pool of a suburban family in Ottawa. And wild turkeys calmly stroll past commuter highways in Virginia.

2. What is happening to the animals around us? Species that were once on the endangered list are making a comeback, thanks to good wildlife management. Not only have many species of animals survived the destruction of their natural habitats, but many of them are now thriving. But while we take pleasure in living with these animals, they can present

inconvenience and even danger. People often confuse what is "normal" for humans with what is normal for animals.

3. Dolphins, for example, have become big business. In the warmer months, Florida tourists pay up to $40 to go on "Dolphin Encounters," " Dolphin Petting Tours," and "Swim with the Dolphins" excursions. Tourists come to see the lovable creatures with their perpetual smiles who rub up against boats, looking for food. The dolphins put on a great show—leaping, bobbing, and doing acrobatics. They have become so tame they will eat out of people's hands—not only frozen fish, but even junk food such as chocolate bars.

4. But conservationists say all of this a disaster waiting to happen. Although no one has been seriously hurt so far, experts fear that it's only a matter of time. "Dolphins are wild animals. Although we have an image of Flipper on TV, in reality dolphins are predators—large, efficient predators" one expert points out. And it's happened already. Dozens of reports have come in from people claiming to have been bitten by dolphins. One woman was hospitalized for a week after she had to rip her leg out of a dolphin's mouth. She needed 20 stitches to close the gash she received after she jumped into the water to swim with a pair of dolphins.

5. But the greatest danger may in fact be to the animals themselves. Dolphins in Florida have died from eating contaminated food, as well as from harassment and injuries inflicted by people attempting to feed them. Feeding the dolphins also changes their routine, so that mother dolphins, accustomed to receiving food from humans, won't teach their young to hunt. Eventually the population will dwindle. And changing their ranging patterns eventually leads some dolphins to leave their groups and become solitary and increasingly aggressive.

6. Bears, who may appear powerful and invulnerable, are also at risk. Because they have few natural predators, they quickly become accustomed to human contact, and are easily lured to vacation spots by city dwellers who feed them scraps of food. The risk to people is obvious. As more and more people invade state and national parks, campers have reported getting dangerous swats from bears they have fed or teased. Bears have been known to turn on people who have fed them, and attack them. But the bears are in danger too. Some that become too trusting are shot. They are also in danger of being hit by cars that travel the roads through the parks.

7. But some stories end on a happy note. Alligators nearly disappeared in the 1960s. For the last 200 years they have been hunted down, out of fear or for profit. Originally numbering in the millions, they were placed on the endangered species list in 1967. Today, protected from their chief predators—humans —alligators are considered completely recovered. Although some alligators are shot legally, monitoring ensures their survival. With a little effort, it seems that people and "gators" can co-exist.

Questions

1. Give three examples of unusual encounters between animals and humans.

2. What has happened to some animals on the endangered species list?

3. In what way are people often confused about wild animals?

4. How do the Florida dolphins act when people come to see them?

5. Why do conservationists think there will be a serious accident one day?

6. What kind of problems have dolphins had as a result of the food people give them?

7. Why is the dolphin population endangered by being fed by people?

8. What has happened to people who feed bears?

9. What are the dangers to bears who trust people?

10. How has the alligator's situation changed recently?

C Use these clues to complete the puzzle. Check the article to find the context for the clues.

Across

2. hunter, killer (paragraph 4)

3. alone, single (paragraph 5)

4. poisonous, toxic (paragraph 5)

6. within the law (paragraph 7)

9. gymnastics (paragraph 3)

11. doing well (paragraph 2)

12. walk slowly (paragraph 1)

13. go into and take over (paragraph 6)

Down

1. money (paragraph 7)

2. continuous (paragraph 3)

5. indestructible (paragraph 6)

7. large cut, laceration (paragraph 4)

8. place animals live (paragraph 2)

10. washing (paragraph 1)

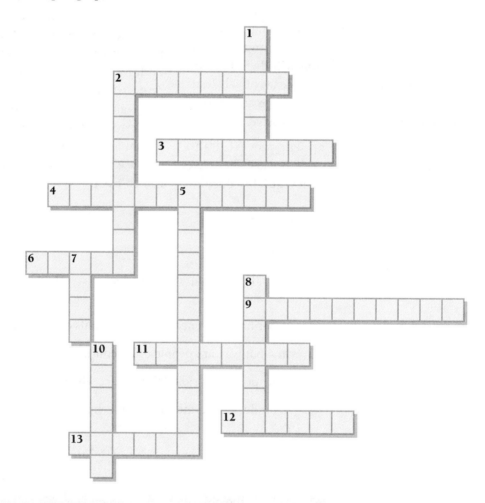

ANIMALS AROUND US

A Read this paragraph. Then close your book and write as the teacher dictates.

By taming, breeding, and caring for wild animals, we have created many domesticated species that enrich our lives. Animals have given us food, clothing, transportation, and entertainment. People have relied on horses for transportation and dogs for companionship, protection, and hunting. Cows have supplied us with meat, dairy products, and leather. Today, domesticated animals do chores for people with disabilities, and even help to clean up the environment.

BIZARRO ©1997 by Dan Piraro. Reprinted with permission of UNIVERSAL PRESS SYNDICATE. All rights reserved.

CANADIAN CAPSULES Cats have always been intelligent animals. There is a story about a cat named Emmy, who made many trips on the ocean liner *The Empress of Ireland*. On May 28, 1914, she refused to board the ship as it prepared to sail from Quebec City to England. That night *The Empress of Ireland* hit another ship in dense fog on the St. Lawrence River, and sank.

B   Read these statements with a partner and decide whether they are true or false.

1.   Horses were the first animals to be tamed.

2.   Birds have been used to send messages for thousands of years.

3.   In the 1850s, rabbits ate all the grass and caused drought in Australia.

4.   Amongst the first animals that people tamed were the animals they ate.

5.   Animals started to appear in movies in the 1950s.

6.   Goldfish became popular pets in Europe, in the 1930s.

7.   Ostriches were nearly wiped out when their feathers became a popular fashion.

8.   The first live Giant Panda in the United States came to San Francisco from China.

9.   Two monkeys that were sent in a rocket into space in 1959 survived the trip.

10.   A dog earned over a million dollars starring in a movie.

11.   A gorilla and a chimpanzee were taught to communicate by speaking.

12.   Pigs were domesticated about 1000 years ago.

13.   People have been keeping bees for over 4000 years.

14.   The first animal to appear in a movie was a cat.

15.   Chickens were first domesticated in North America.

16.   People have been raising silkworms for silk for at least 3000 years.

C   Consult the time line at the bottom of pages 52–55 to check your answers.

Time Line

People began to tame the animals they ate. In different parts of the world, cattle such as the cow, reindeer, yak, and llama were domesticated.

Horses were ridden by humans. They were used later to carry and pull loads.

| Stone Ages | 12 000 Years Ago | 8000 Years Ago | 6000 Years Ago |

Dogs were the first animals to be tamed. People used them to hunt animals for food.

Pigs were domesticated.

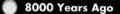

ANIMAL PARTNERS

 LISTENING ACTIVITY 4 *Interview with Charles Benson, Writer*

 A Match the parts of the animals to the pictures.

1. wing
2. mane
3. hoof
4. tail
5. paw
6. snout
7. udder
8. claw
9. fur
10. feathers
11. beak
12. horns

Chickens were first domesticated in Southeast Asia. They were used for their meat and for eggs.

Common people (i.e., not nobles or royalty) in China were allowed to raise silkworms for silk.

5000 Years Ago   **4500 Years Ago**   **2630 BC**   **1103 BC**

In ancient Egypt, cats were worshipped because they protected grain from rats and mice.

Egyptians left records about bee keeping on temple walls.

The sultan of Baghdad had a pigeon postal system, with birds being used to send messages.

B Read the questions with a partner. Then listen and answer the questions. Use the worksheet.

1. Why does Charles call the cow a vending machine?

2. Which animals were the first to become domesticated?

3. Why did wolves probably start coming closer to humans?

4. How did the wolves produce different species?

5. How did we get the dogs we know today?

6. When did cats become important to people?

7. Why were cats treated like royalty?

8. What are some things dogs do to help humans?

9. How do capuchin monkeys help people who are paralyzed or in wheelchairs?

10. How do we know dolphins are intelligent?

11. Why have dolphins been used as retriever dogs of the sea?

12. Why are dolphins used as guards?

13. How might the spider be used in the future?

 **GRAMMAR FOCUS** ── **Indefinite Pronouns**

Indefinite pronouns refer to a person, thing, or place without being specific. Pronouns that end with **one** or **body** refer to people and have the same meaning. The indefinite pronoun **no one** is written as two words.

everyone	someone	anyone	no one
everybody	somebody	anybody	nobody
everything	something	anything	nothing
everywhere	somewhere	anywhere	nowhere

Ostrich feathers became the rage. Women wore the tall feathers in their hats and around their necks. These styles wiped out almost the entire ostrich population in North Africa.

Pet shops in New York City sold thousands of gold-fish. This craze for goldfish begin when P.T. Barnum displayed them at his circus in 1850.

The dog Rin Tin Tin, a German Shepherd who starred in the movies, was the first animal to earn over a million dollars.

●1800s   ●1859   ●1865   ●1902   ●1925

Twenty-four rabbits arrived in Australia, and were set free on a ranch. Three years later, millions of rabbits had turned thousands of kilometres of pasture into dust.

The first animal to star in a movie was Rover, a collie, who appeared in *Rescue by Rover*.

Use a singular form of the verb when an indefinite pronoun is the subject of a sentence.

> **Somebody** is at the door.
>
> **Everybody** is tired today.

Use **everyone/everybody** or **everything** to refer to all members of a group.

> **Everyone** is here now. (Ann, Max, Lili, etc.)
>
> **Everything** is ready for the party. (music, food, etc.)

Use **someone/somebody** or **something** in affirmative statements or in questions where you expect an affirmative answer.

> **Someone** (I don't know who) left the door to the cage open.
>
> Would you like something (peanuts, lettuce, etc.) to feed the bear?

Use **anyone/anybody** or **anything** in negative statements or in questions where you aren't sure of the answer.

> I didn't know **anything** about dolphins.
>
> Did **anyone** remember to bring a camera?

Use **no one/nobody** or **nothing** to refer to the absence of a person or thing.

> I got home and noticed that **nobody** (not my sister, not my father, not my mother, etc.) had fed the cat.
>
> The newspapers said **nothing** (not that it was caught, not that it had cubs, etc.) about the brown bear.

Able and Baker, two monkeys, survived being sent into space in a rocket.

Koko was the first gorilla to learn American sign language for the deaf.

1936   **1959**   **1966**   **1977**

Su-Lin was the first live Giant Panda to be seen in the United States. She was brought to San Francisco from China.

Washoe was the first chimpanzee to learn to communicate in words. She was taught the American sign language for the deaf.

Do not use these pronouns **if the verb is negative**.

> ✗ He didn't say nothing.
> ✔ He said **nothing**.
> ✔ He didn't say **anything**.

A   Choose the correct indefinite pronoun to complete the sentence. In some cases more than one indefinite pronoun is possible.

1.   The polar bear isn't in the cage. I can't see it _____.

2.   Did you remember to bring _____ to feed the animals?

3.   I really enjoyed the zoo, but _____ agreed with me.

4.   We went whale-watching but _____ had a camera.

5.   They looked for the giant panda, but they couldn't see it _____.

6.   Did _____ think about how the wild animals were feeling?

7.   The animals look hungry, but I don't have _____ to give them.

8.   _____ is responsible for leaving the door to the monkeys' cage open.

9.   Will the public notice that _____ is wrong at the zoo?

10. Can you contribute to the campaign? _____ you can give will be appreciated.

B   Find the errors in the sentences and correct them.

1.   The papers didn't say nothing about the problem at the zoo.

2.   Nobody are responsible for the difficulties we have had recently.

3.   Someone knows that a bear is a dangerous wild animal.

4.   Franco didn't see no one when he checked the area near the pool.

5.   When Ann asked for help, anybody was ready to help her.

6.   Everything are in good order for the performance tomorrow.

7.   If they don't have it there, I can try anywhere else in the store.

8.   Caroline didn't notice whether nothing else was missing or not.

9.   Everyone else were at work first thing in the morning.

10. Nobody were there when the accident took place yesterday.

WHOSE JOB IS IT?

 Read this story with a partner, just for fun!

This is a story about four people named Everybody, Somebody, Anybody, and Nobody.

There was an important job to be done and Everybody was sure Somebody would do it. Anybody could have done it, but Nobody did it. Somebody got angry about that because it was Everybody's job. Everybody thought Anybody could do it, but Nobody realized that Everybody couldn't do it. It ended up that Everybody blamed Somebody when Nobody did what Anybody could have done!

CINNAMON BEAR

CBC VIDEO ACTIVITY 2

A Discuss these questions in a group.

1. Why do you think that people want to get close to wild animals?

2. Can you think of any animals that became famous?

3. What problems can develop when a wild animal becomes a celebrity?

B   Read the questions with a partner. Then watch the video and answer the questions. Use the worksheet.

1. How long has Fulka been in the Maleen Valley?

2. What image do bears project?

3. What is the biggest privilege to Fulka?

4. What are the guests excited about?

5. Where are the guests from?

6. How does Fulka feel when he sees the bear?

7. Describe the pictures taken of the bears by:
   a) their daughter
   b) their friend Don Jones

8. How is the cinnamon bear described?

9. What happens when a lot of people come to see the bears?

10. What is the danger to people and animals when tourists stop to see the bears?

11. Why is the cinnamon bear under stress?

12. What happened to her cubs three years ago?

13. How did the young cub die?

14. What balance do we have to find between people and bears?

15. What do we learn from observing bears?

16. What will happen if there is more development of the parks?

IN MY OPINION

Man's Best Friend

Discuss these questions in a group and explain your answers.

1. Which animals do you think are most suited to living with people?

2. How are pets in North America treated differently from animals in other parts of the world?

3. How have human beings contributed to the extinction of animal species?

4. How much time, effort, and money do you feel should be spent in keeping animal species from becoming extinct?

5. If you had the power to save any species of animal from extinction, which one would you choose?

Up for Debate

A   Choose one topic and prepare to debate.

1. There should be restrictions on the number of pets allowed in one household.

2. It is morally indefensible to use animals to develop and test new products.

3. The public should make efforts to preserve as many animal species as possible.

    B   Choose one of the topics and write about it. Give information and examples to defend your point of view.

SHARPEN YOUR ENGLISH

Vocabulary

    Which of the following **animal** expressions have equivalents in your language? Work in a group to discuss these expressions.

1. The couple we were talking to last night were real **birdbrains**. (stupid)

2. Maria made a really **catty** remark about her friend's dress. (jealous, nasty)

3. Paul felt embarrassed. He just **clammed up**. (refused to say anything)

4. Jean-Pierre wouldn't try skiing because he was **chicken**. (afraid)

5. The worst thing to do if you need money is go to a **loan shark**. (money lender)

6. Mario is always reading. He is a real **bookworm**. (enjoys reading)

7. Don't trust that man. He is **as slippery as an eel**. (dishonest)

8. The younger brother was always **aping** his sister's behavior. (copying)

9. He is a real **pig** when it comes to housekeeping. (messy, dirty)

10. Be careful. There is something **fishy** about that person. (suspicious)

11. She doesn't have much personality. She's kind of **mousy**. (timid, shy)

12. This is serious; you should stop **monkeying** around. (fooling)

13. What a party! Everyone had a **whale** of a time. (wonderful)

14. Suzanna has been **squirreling** away her money for ages. (saving)

15. Joe was careful because he smelled a **rat**. (something wrong)

IT'S AGAINST THE LAW

WATCH OUT FOR SCAMS!

A Discuss and answer these questions with a partner.

1. What is white-collar crime? Give an example.

2. Why has white-collar crime increased lately?

3. What is a "scam"?

4. Why are more and more people becoming victims of scams?

B Read the paragraphs quickly and add information to your answers.

Originally, "white-collar crime" referred to acts committed by business and professional people while earning their living. It included crimes such as stock market swindles and other types of fraud. But the increase of computers has created new opportunities for white-collar crime. Computer crimes are easy to commit by clever criminals who learn how a system works, but they are difficult to detect.

Other types of white-collar crimes include "scams," ways of cheating people that may not actually be illegal. Scams may be based on misleading or ambiguous claims. They are designed to get your money by appealing to your desire to get something for nothing. Today's sophisticated technology offers scam artists new opportunities to reach victims through the touch of a dial or a keyboard. You don't even have to leave your house to become a target. Some scams are merely annoying, while others have tragic consequences. If you know what to look out for, however, you can protect yourself from white-collar crimes and scams.

A Here are some common scenarios. You have probably experienced a few yourself. In a group, read them and discuss what to do.

1. You receive a notice in the mail that says you have won a terrific gift. All you have to do is call a special number to confirm your eligibility. Should you go out and celebrate your new-found fortune?

2. You see an ad for a VCR priced at $200. When you get to the store, you find that there are no VCRs left at that price, but there is another model which costs $150 more. You were planning to buy a VCR. Should you buy the more expensive one?

3. You are informed by phone or mail that you have definitely won one of several large prizes which include a new car, a computer, and a diamond ring. All you have to do is pay a small fee to qualify. Should you sell your old car and get ready for the new one?

4. You receive a postcard offering a free gift. All you have to do is return the card. You don't especially want the product, but it's free. Should you return the card?

5. A sales person comes to your house selling encyclopedias. The encyclopedias look great, so you buy a set and pay right away. The next day you change your mind. Are you stuck with the encyclopedias?

6. You are in a shopping centre and see a shiny red sports car, with a big sign saying "Win Me!" All you have to do is complete an entry form with your name, address, telephone number, age, sex, and family income. You picture yourself driving down the highway this summer in your shiny new car. Should you fill in a few extra forms, since it only takes a few minutes and might increase your chances of winning?

7. You join a health club and are encouraged to purchase a life-time membership. You are told that you can save a lot of money if you pay the life-time membership immediately rather than the monthly membership fee. You really want to get in shape and this sounds like a good deal. Should you pay?

8. You are buying a used car and the salesperson assures you the car is good for another 30 000 kilometers without trouble. Should you believe the salesperson?

9. In the mail, you receive goods that you did not order. Are you obliged to return them or pay for them?

10. You arrive in a new city and call home from a phone booth in the airport, using a calling card. You talk for a few minutes and assume the call costs about $10. A few weeks later you receive a bill for several hundred dollars. What happened?

 B Turn to page 74 to check your answers.

CANADIAN CAPSULES

In a recent survey, over 60 percent of Canadians said neither they nor a close family member had been a victim of crime. About 13 percent said they personally had been a victim of crime.

HOW A THIEF STOLE MY NAME

  A   With a partner, discuss the questions below. Then complete the chart.

1.   Which of these items listed do you carry when you go out every day?

2.   What would be the immediate effect on you if you lost each one?

3.   How would you replace each one?

4.   How much time do you think it would cost to replace each one?

Item	Carry (Yes/No)	Effect of losing	Way of replacing	Time to replace
keys				
cash				
credit card				
medical-insurance card				
diver's licence				
bank card				
chequebook				
social insurance card				

B   Skim the story on pages 65 and 66 and put the steps below in the correct order; a) is number 1.

a) Marcia Vickers went to Lucky's Restaurant and had her purse stolen.

b) She was careful with her bag and stopped carrying credit cards.

c) She had a locksmith put a new lock on the door of her apartment.

d) The store detective let the fake Marcia Vickers walk away from the store.

e) The police told her that the other Marcia was likely a professional thief.

f) She canceled 15 credit and department-store cards that she had.

g) A store detective stopped the other Marcia when she tried to open an account.

h) She dashed to the bank and canceled her ATM card and chequing account.

i) She changed the message on her answering machine to warn people.

j) She issued a fraud report to the major credit-reporting bureaus.

How A Thief Stole My Name

Marcia Vickers

A. I am the real Marcia Vickers. I swear. Ever since my tote bag was snatched in a restaurant—and with it my chequebook, credit cards, driver's licence and keys—there has been some confusion about this. For a time another woman became me. For months she worked assorted shopping centres, using my credit to create new accounts and leaving a trail of unpaid bills and angry retailers behind. Then, having played out the value of my identity, my alter ego moved on, possibly mutating into someone else.

B. I was, in short, a victim of what police call "true-name" or "account takeover" fraud, an increasingly troublesome category of white-collar crime. It was a grueling experience. Having made the trip, though, I have some lessons to impart.

C. True-name fraud is big business these days. One expert estimates that last year world-wide fraud involving bank-issued credit cards amounted to $3.9 billion. The growth in computer use is also partly to blame, adding elements of speed to financial fraud. The result is a different and more dangerous criminal. Once thieves get their hands on enough of a person's identification, they are not limited to credit-card fraud. They can sin in myriad ways, from forging cheques to accessing your account.

D. I did not know any of this when my ordeal began in September 1994. After a leisurely lunch with my editor at a restaurant named—what else?—Lucky's, I reached down to retrieve my bag from the floor. It was gone. I felt sick. My monetary loss was negligible, but my life—just about everything that defined me—had been in that bag. My editor and I hurried back to the office, where I immediately called and canceled my 15 credit and department-store cards. Next I dashed to my bank and canceled my ATM card and chequing account. Then I raced to my apartment and had a locksmith change the dead bolt on my door.

E. Later in the week I got word of the other Marcia. I called the major credit-reporting bureaus and had them place a fraud alert on my credit records. But that merely instructed creditors to call me personally to verify applicant information. As the other Marcia opened one instant-charge account after another, store detectives would call to confirm that the Marcia Vickers who was applying for credit was indeed me. But just reaching my answering machine was enough for some to give "Marcia" the green light.

Hello...This is Marcia Vickers....

F. Being a victim of this kind of fraud was just plain hard work. My alter ego got lots of merchandise and cash: I got to clean up the mess she left behind. For months I spent up to ten hours a week trying to contain the problem—phoning, writing and dealing with retailers, card issuers, agencies and the police. I had to deconstruct myself and then rebuild, canceling one account after another so I could start anew.

G. For six months after the loss of my bag, I made myself as theftproof as I could. At all times I was careful about where I placed my bag. I stopped carrying my chequebook, I took only two credit cards with me, leaving the rest at home. To stop the other Marcia from opening more charge accounts, I finally came up with a new greeting for my answering machine: "This is Marcia Vickers. My wallet was recently stolen, and someone claiming to be me is trying to establish credit using this telephone number.... " To my surprise, this worked. Store and police detectives praised my ingenuity. "Great message!" they'd say, or "Ms. Vickers, thank you, you've just answered my questions."

H. My hopes soared the day a detective called to tell me "Marcia" was in a store trying to open a charge account. "She'll be nabbed and her paper trail will finally stop," I foolishly thought. I asked him to describe her. "Black hair that looks like it's dyed orange," he said in a low voice. "She's wearing a pink sweat suit, and she has lots of gold jewelry and a gold tooth." Because the detective reached me before my impostor made the purchase, the store would not let her complete the sale. But because she did not get any merchandise, the store would not have her arrested. She walked away. The nightmare continued. After several months one of the detectives on the case told me that the police had tentatively identified the other Marcia as a member of a professional theft ring. But she was never arrested. I may be living with the other Marcia for a long time.

C Read the story carefully and answer the questions.

1. What is "true-name" fraud? How does it work?

2. What does the figure $3.9 billion represent?

3. Why did Marcia Vickers feel sick when she realized her purse had been stolen?

4. What resulted from the fraud alert? Was the alert effective?

5. How does Marcia support her claim that being the victim of fraud is hard work?

6. How did people react to the new answering-machine message?

7. What news made Marcia's hopes soar?

8. What did the fake Marcia look like?

9. Explain why the store didn't have the fake Marcia arrested.

10. What did the police finally tell Marcia about the thief?

D Build your vocabulary by finding these words in the story.

1. Paragraph A: List the nouns that follow **my**.

2. Paragraphs B & C: List adjectives that precede the word **fraud**.

3. Paragraph D: Find three words that mean **rushed**.

4. Paragraph E: Find two words that mean **make certain**.

5. Paragraph F: Name four people the real Marcia had to deal with.

6. Paragraph G: How did Marcia make herself **theftproof**? Use your own words.

7. Paragraph H: Give another word for **arrested** and another word for **sale**.

WHAT'S YOUR EXPERIENCE?

Write about a white-collar crime or scam that you know about. It could be something that happened to you or someone you know or something you learned about from the news. Explain how the crime happened and the effect it had on the victims.

There is a Canada-wide anti-fraud operation that is run by the Ontario Provincial Police. You can call collect to report anyone who calls to tell you that you have won money but must send a cheque to receive it. The number is (705) 495-8501.

LISTENING ACTIVITY **5**   *Interview with Police Detective Dan Bumbridge*

A   Look at the pictures. With your group, discuss what you see.

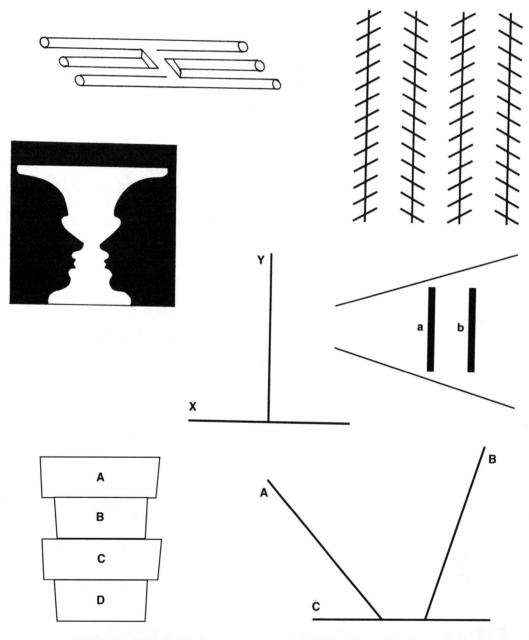

B Listen to identify the main idea.

1. Most people are poor witnesses because they don't have good memories.

2. Eye-witnesses are important in helping police officers to solve crimes

3. Many factors can influence how accurately witnesses observe events.

4. More criminals would go to jail if more people were willing to be witnesses.

C Read the questions. Then listen again and answer the questions. Use the worksheet.

1. What was wrong with the descriptions of the robber that witnesses gave the police?

2. What conflicting information was given about the get-away car?

3. How does the police detective explain the details the shopkeeper remembered about the robber?

4. What was each of the following witnesses focusing on at the time of the robbery?
   a) the couple going out to dinner
   b) the young man outside the store
   c) the woman who was entering the store

5. What details did the following people recall about the woman outside the café?
   a) the first person
   b) the second person
   c) the child

6. How long do our memories retain details?

7. What three things can alter our memory of details?

8. What are three physical impediments that can affect our visual perception?

9. How long does it take the eye to adjust to darkness?

10. Why was the detective happy to appear on the program?

 **Conditional Sentences: Types I and II**

A conditional sentence shows an **if/then** relationship between two actions. Conditional clauses contain **if** and describe an action or state that must happen in order for another action (or state) to occur. We call the **if** clause the **conditional clause**, and the main clause the **result clause**.

Conditional I expresses the **if** clause in the present tense and the result clause in future time.

> If you rob a bank, you will go to jail.

Conditional II expresses the **if** clause in past time and the main clause with **would** + the base form of the main verb.

> If you stole money, you would be a thief.

Match the sentences to make conditional sentences.

1. If you leave your keys in your car,
2. If you report a burglary,
3. If the police catch a bank robber,
4. If a robber doesn't wear a mask,
5. If someone steals your wallet,
6. If you see a crime being committed,
7. If a victim has insurance on her property,
8. If a criminal is arrested,
9. If nobody sees a crime being committed,
10. If you are careful,

a) she will be compensated.
b) you will be a witness to the crime.
c) the police will investigate.
d) you will lose your money.
e) there will be no witnesses.
f) they will arrest him.
g) someone will probably steal it.
h) you probably won't be robbed.
i) he will go to court.
j) he will be recognized.

B   Choose the correct clause to complete these sentences logically.

1. If you aren't careful,
   a) you won't be robbed.
   b) you will be robbed.

2. If you are a witness,
   a) you won't appear in court.
   b) you will appear in court.

3. If you don't have a credit card,
   a) you won't pay cash.
   b) you will pay cash.

4. If the police are on strike,
   a) there will be more robberies.
   b) there won't be more robberies.

5. If you aren't careful in a crowd,
   a) a pickpocket will take your wallet.
   b) a pickpocket won't take your wallet.

6. If they hear a burglar alarm,
   a) the police won't investigate.
   b) the police will investigate.

7. If the store detective catches a shoplifter,
   a) she will probably call the police.
   b) she probably won't call the police.

8. If a criminal goes to court,
   a) he will need a lawyer.
   b) he won't need a lawyer.

9.　If there is no witness to a crime,

a)　it won't be hard to get a conviction.

b)　it will be hard to get a conviction.

10.　If you don't pay your credit card bill on time,

a)　you won't need to pay interest.

b)　you will need to pay interest.

C　Complete the Conditional II sentences by using the correct form of the verb in brackets.

1.　If I _____ (get) into debt, I would cut up my credit cards.

2.　If I lost my credit card, I _____ (call) the police to report it.

3.　If you lived in the city, you _____ (be) more likely to get robbed.

4.　If banks _____ (have) better security, they wouldn't be robbed so often.

5.　If she _____ (apply) for a credit card, her application would be accepted.

6.　If he _____ (lose) his credit card, he would report it immediately.

7.　If they were honest, they _____ (not try) to cheat people.

8.　If anyone _____ (report) a crime, the police would investigate.

9.　If I had more time, I _____ (install) a burglar alarm.

10.　If someone _____ (steal) your car, you would report it at once.

IN MY OPINION

Why Do They Do It?

People commit crimes for many reasons. For example, a person who doesn't have enough to eat might steal food, while a drug addict might steal money to pay for narcotics.

A   Work in a group. Talk about each of the following criminals. Who is most likely to commit the crime? Who is the most likely victim? What are the most likely reasons people commit this crime?

B   Write your conclusions in a chart similar to the one below. When you have finished, compare your information with that of other groups in the class.

	Type of person	Most likely reasons	Most likely victim
a shoplifter			
an embezzler			
a bank robber			
a car thief			
a kidnapper			
a con artist			
an arsonist			
a vandal			
a forger			
a smuggler			
an assassin			
a juvenile delinquent			
a skyjacker			

SHARPEN YOUR ENGLISH

Vocabulary

The list below shows some words that deal with different kinds of crimes. Some crimes are committed against people or property. Other crimes are committed against public order or morality. Some are classified as indictable offences, which are more serious crimes. Others are summary conviction offences, which are generally considered less serious crimes.

Work with a partner.

1. Select five words that are **new to you**, from the list below. Check the words in the dictionary. Then discuss what kind of crime it is, who is likely to commit the crime, and what you think the punishment should be.

2. Write a small paragraph about each of the five crimes. Compare your information with that of other groups.

fraud	assault
arson	blackmail
counterfeiting	bribery
vagrancy	breach of promise
homicide	forgery
larceny	embezzlement
libel	slander
manslaughter	smuggling
conspiracy	sabotage
burglary	treason
bigamy	vandalism
contempt	shoplifting

WHAT'S GOING ON?

Read the paragraphs to find the answers to the questions on pages 62 and 63.

1. You may be charged $3-$4 per minute for this telephone call, which may turn out to be far more than the gift is worth.

2. This is an old game, but somehow stores still manage to get away with it. It is against the law to advertise items when there is insufficient supply, and then try to get customers to buy a similar, higher-priced item. You should be able to buy the advertised item later, at the price stated.

3. Most of the winners receive the diamond ring, which turns out to be a tiny diamond chip, worth less than the small fee you paid.

4. You may be sent a bill for a second or third similar item. You also may find you are now enrolled in a club, such as a book-of-the-month or tape-of-the-month club, where you are obliged to buy a certain number of items per year.

5. There are laws to protect you from aggressive sales people who come to your door pushing vacuum cleaners or encyclopedias. If you do buy something, there is a time lapse of a few days, during which you can change your mind after you sign a contract.

6. What you receive may not be a shiny new red car— it may be junk mail. When you fill out forms with your age, sex, and income, you give out a lot of information about yourself. Businesses pay top dollar to get mailing lists for their target audiences. So in setting up a contest like this, companies actually make their money by generating mailing lists.

7. It's not a good idea to pay in advance for services such as health clubs. Many health or leisure clubs have gone out of business, and people who paid in advance have lost money. Before you join a health club, check out the company very carefully to make sure it has a good track record.

8. An oral contract is just as valid as a written warranty, but it will carry more weight if you have a witness to back you up. To be safe, it's best to have a written contract.

9. If you receive unsolicited merchandise in the mail, you are not obliged to pay for it or to return the item.

10. You are a victim of a "shoulder surfer." These people watch a caller punch in a number by looking over the caller's shoulder, by using binoculars, or by taping the caller on a camcorder as they walk by. They then sell the caller's number to people who market stolen numbers. Someone can buy your number and get free long-distance calls, at your expense.

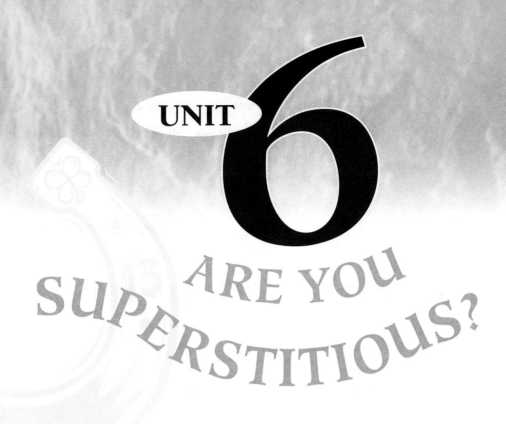

UNIT 6
ARE YOU SUPERSTITIOUS?

GOOD LUCK AND BAD LUCK

  A Work with a partner. Use the words below to complete the paragraphs.

**nature win existed mistake socks charm
exam weather lucky page lesson**

Do you believe in good luck and bad luck? Many people today say they don't believe in __1_____ signs, and that superstitions are silly. Yet how many people do you know who buy lottery tickets and choose "lucky numbers," hoping to __2_____ money?

Superstition has always been part of human __3_____ and has __4_____ in every society. There are superstitions about numbers, animals, food, the __5_____, the sky, illness, work, sleep, and parts of the body.

There are even superstitions about being a good student. For example, to help you learn your __6_____, sleep with your book under your pillow. Just be sure the book is open to the right __7_____! And to succeed on an __8_____, follow these simple steps: wear your __9_____ and underwear inside out, and your shirt or blouse backwards. Carry a lucky __10_____ with you, and use a new pen or pencil that has never made a __11_____.

77

B   Discuss these questions in a group.

1.   Do you think of yourself as superstitious? If not, why not?

2.   Is anyone you know, such as a family member or neighbour, superstitious?

3.   What are some superstitions or beliefs that you know about?

4.   If you have any superstitions, do you know their origins?

WHAT DO YOU BELIEVE?

Many of the superstitions and rituals we follow today come from the past. Do you know where these common superstitions come from?

A   Work in a group to choose the best answers to the quiz.

1.   Which number is bad luck in Asia?
     a)   4
     b)   13
     c)   3

2.   Opening an umbrella indoors was thought to be bad luck because:
     a) it would cause rain
     b) it could injure someone
     c) umbrellas broke easily

3.   Which of these animals brings good luck?
     a)   the rabbit
     b)   the mouse
     c)   the cat

4.   What should you do with a horseshoe to bring you good luck?
     a)   throw it
     b)   nail it to your front door
     c)   give it to a farmer

5.   According to superstition, which day is the most important of the year?
     a)   Christmas
     b)   New Year's day
     c)   Easter

6. Which of these things will not bring bad luck?

   a) walking under a ladder

   b) wearing a sweater inside out

   c) breaking a mirror

7. Which **two** of these things tell you company is coming?

   a) dropping a knife or fork

   b) sneezing after dinner

   c) pouring a glass of water with bubbles in it

8. Which of these brings good luck?

   a) a daisy

   b) a pine cone

   c) a four-leaf clover

9. Which bird is said to bring babies?

   a) the robin

   b) the stork

   c) the swallow

10. You can tell if someone is gossiping about you if:

    a) the palms of your hands itch

    b) your eyelids twitch

    c) your ears ring

11. Which animal is said to see the future?

    a) the owl

    b) the bear

    c) the spider

12. Which flower is useful if you have a question about the future?

    a) the rose

    b) the daisy

    c) the tulip

B Read the text quickly to find the answers to the quiz.

What Do You Believe?

In the past, people had no scientific explanations for events they didn't understand, such as birth, thunderstorms, and changes in the weather. They thought that these events were caused by spirits, and they developed ways to welcome the good spirits and chase away the evil ones.

Over the years, many everyday objects and practices took on special meaning. The belief that it is bad luck to open an umbrella in the house began in Europe many years ago, when umbrellas were difficult to open and close. Opening an umbrella in a small space could cause injuries or damage. In the same way, walking under a ladder could be dangerous because something could fall on you.

People fear that if they break a mirror they will have seven years of bad luck. This superstition may have begun with people gazing at their reflections in a lake. When the wind rippled the water, the image was shattered, and this meant bad luck. This was probably how people felt when they broke a mirror. Wearing an item of clothing backwards, or inside out, is considered good luck. So if, by mistake, you walk under a ladder or break a mirror, you can try to reverse your bad luck by the way you wear your clothes!

Four-leaf clovers are rare, so finding one brings good luck. To improve your luck even more, wear it in your shoe. Daisies and dandelions are useful too. If you have a question about the future, pull off the petals of a daisy one by one, saying "yes" and "no" alternately.

The last petal will give you the answer you are seeking.

In North America, the number 13 is considered unlucky. In fact, there is even a name for the fear of the number 13: triskaidekaphobia. Many buildings in North America do not have a 13th floor. The apartment floor or number that should be number 13 is given a different number. The reason for thinking of 13 as bad luck is uncertain. In Japan, China, and Korea 13 is not thought to be bad luck, but the number 4 is. This is because the character for the number 4, "shi," sounds like the word for "death." So in Tokyo, Taipei, or Seoul many buildings have no 4th floor.

Humans have always lived with animals and depended on them for transportation, protection, and food. Rabbits bring good luck because they produce many children. Owls, on the other hand, bring bad luck because they hoot and screech, which means disaster is on its way. Not only that: owls can also see in the dark, which means they know the future. In Scandinavia, the stork was said to bring babies because it was a gentle bird that took good care of its young. It returned to the same chimney year after year to build its nest. This led to the expression "the stork came," which is used to announce the birth of a baby.

The shoe of a horse is considered lucky, but this has nothing to do with the horse. The horseshoe is made of iron, which was a sacred metal. In addition, the shape resembles a crescent moon, a sign of protection from evil. In some countries, church doors were built in the shape of a crescent moon or a horseshoe. For this reason, nailing a horseshoe to your front door will bring you good luck.

Days and dates are also important. New Year's day is the most important day of the year, because it influences the rest of the year. To ensure good luck, you must remember that the way you behave on this day will be the way you behave all year. Some people also try to be kissed on this day. If no one kisses you on New Year's day, you will have to wait another year!

Finally, you can tell if someone is talking about you if your ears tingle or ring. If your right ear rings, people are saying something good, but if it is your left ear, they are saying something bad. And if you drop a knife or fork, sneeze before breakfast, or pour a glass of water with bubbles in it, you'd better get ready for company!

WHY DO YOU DO THAT?

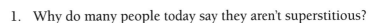

LISTENING ACTIVITY 6   *Interview with Steven Woods, Writer*

Read the questions aloud with a partner. Then listen and answer the questions. Use the worksheet.

1. Why do many people today say they aren't superstitious?

2. What are some things people do today to bring good luck?

3. What are some events people could not understand or control?

4. What did they think was responsible for these events?

5. Why was salt so valuable in the past?

6. What did spilled salt signify?

7. Which group of people have invented new superstitions recently?

8. Give examples of some rituals that baseball players follow.

9. What are some events that are surrounded by rituals?

10. Why did brides originally begin to wear veils?

11. Why do people continue to have rituals today?

Reporting Verbs: "Say" and "Tell"

The most common reporting verbs are **say** and **tell**. Use **say** (**said**) when there is no mention of the person to whom the speaker was talking.

> Burhan **says** that he believes in ghosts.

Use **tell** (**told**) when you mention the person to whom the speaker was talking.

> Burhan **told me** that he believes in ghosts.

 Change the verb **say** to **tell** and identify the person to whom the speaker was talking. Use the correct tense (present or past).

> She **said** that she was worried. (her friend)
> She **told her friend** that she was worried.

1. Manuel said that he thought superstitions were silly. (the group)

2. Maria says that her grandmother is superstitious. (us)

3. The speaker said that rituals make people feel in control. (the audience)

4. Someone said that baseball players have many strange rituals. (me)

5. Tom says that he isn't really superstitious. (our friends)

6. My neighbour says that killing a spider brings rain. (me)

7. Min Hee said that she thinks the number 4 is unlucky. (all of us)

8. Susan said that she believes the number 13 is unlucky. (Min Hee)

9. Hiroshi says that many buildings in Tokyo don't have a fourth floor. (Tina)

10. Some people say that black cats can bring bad luck. (their children)

Some people carry a rabbit's foot for good luck. This practice comes from ancient times, when people believed that rabbits had magical powers because they had so many young. People thought that if they carried a part of the animal, they too would have many children.

B   Complete the sentences by adding a suitable object from the list below. Use each object once.

**her students   the viewers   the children   my brother and me
the hostess   our class   the readers   the tourists   the passengers
the audience**

1. The newspaper reporter told _____ that many Halloween customs came from the past.

2. The dinner guest told _____ that throwing salt over her left shoulder would bring good luck.

3. The elevator operator told _____ that there was no thirteenth floor in this building.

4. The teacher told _____ that it was unlucky to open an umbrella when you were inside.

5. My grandmother told _____ that she knew someone who had really seen a ghost.

6. The TV news reporter told _____ that some people had seen a flying saucer land on their farm.

7. The storyteller told _____ many tales of ghosts and witches just before the school closed for Halloween.

8. The tour guide told _____ that local people believed that the castle was haunted by ghosts.

9. The speaker told _____ that villagers in many parts of the world still believe in magic.

10. The anthropology professor told _____ that many strange beliefs have their roots in real events.

C   Choose **say** or **tell** and put it in the appropriate tense.

1. The guide _____ us not to worry if we heard strange noises.

2. I always _____ what I think no matter what other people believe.

3. Everyone _____ that we would enjoy the trip to the haunted house.

4. Some people _____ us that ghosts lived there and we should be careful.

5. My grandmother _____ that we should wear green on St. Patrick's Day.

6. My father _____ that you shouldn't believe everything you hear.

7. The farmer _____ the reporter that he had seen a flying saucer land there.

8. Mike usually _____ people what he thinks even if they don't ask him.

9. The speaker _____ that superstitions were alive and well even today.

10. We always _____ our friends about our experiences with superstitions.

THE *FARMER'S ALMANAC*

 CBC

 VIDEO ACTIVITY 3

 A Do you think it is possible to predict the future? Work in a group to discuss the items below. Which of these things have you used, or would you use, to tell the future?

1. horoscopes in newspapers or magazines
2. tea leaves
3. a fortune teller or clairvoyant
4. tarot cards
5. the *Farmer's Almanac*
6. a palm reader
7. a numerologist
8. other (Explain.)

 B Read the questions. Then watch the video and answer the questions. Use the worksheet.

1. What does the *Farmer's Almanac* contain?
2. How many copies are sold every year?
3. Why do most of us want to know the weather?
4. What do farmers need to know?
5. What kinds of things does the *Farmer's Almanac* tell?
6. What is it best known for?
7. How accurate does Perry Pierce think it is?
8. For how long has the *Farmer's Almanac* published weather predictions?

9. Where is the secret formula kept?

10. Which three places did the reporter go to ask about the black box?

11. Where does Judson Hale keep the black box?

12. What weather was predicted for December 11–14 in southern Ontario?

13. What actually happened?

14. Why was Judson Hale pleased with his prediction?

15. How do weather forecasters predict the weather?

16. How accurate does Judson Hale say the *Almanac* is?

17. What does the Almanac use to make predictions that the meteorologists don't use?

18. What else does the *Almanac* rely on?

19. What does the weather forecaster think is in the black box?

IN MY OPINION

Is Everybody Superstitious?

A Work in a group. Talk about superstitions in different cultures.

Make a chart and list the superstitions you discuss in the following categories. Then interview people in other groups to add to your chart.

food and drink			
the sky			
numbers and dates			
good-luck charms			
bad-luck signs			
colours			
holidays			
clothing			
animals			
money			
weddings			
ailments and cures			

B   Write about customs and beliefs in your culture regarding special events, such as weddings or holidays.

SHARPEN YOUR ENGLISH

Plurals

Some words that end with the letter **f** have another form (a plural or other verb form) that is made by changing **f** to **v** and adding **es**. The short vowel is then pronounced as a long vowel.

> Example: belief   believes

Work in pairs. Write the plurals and take turns pronouncing both words.

1. life
2. half
3. wife
4. wolf
5. leaf

6. shelf
7. knife
8. thief
9. calf
10. loaf

Spelling and Pronunciation

English words with the letters **ie** or **ei** together are sometimes difficult to spell. In many cases, this rule helps:

> Put **I** before **E** except after **C**
>
> Or when sounded like **A**
>
> As in **neighbour** or **weigh**

One of the words in bold type in each sentence is not spelled correctly. Find the words that are spelled incorrectly. Correct the errors.

1. Most people don't really **beleive** that ghosts are the **chief** danger facing human **beings**.

2. Susan didn't know how to tell her **friends** that the timing of **their** visit was not really **conveneint**.

3. Lola's greatest **achievemen**t as an actress was the role she **received** a prize for at the **Foriegn** Film Festival.

4. The child **believed** that Santa Clause came **quietly** in the night and brought presents in a **sliegh**.

5. You can **retrieve** the goods you are expecting at the **frieght** depot if you have the proper **receipt**.

6. The king couldn't **concieve** of dying without an **heir** who could **reign** over the kingdom after him.

7. The Supernatural **Society** had a **brief** meeting last night to discuss the members' recent **expereinces**.

8. People in the village **beleived** that ghosts and goblins lived in the **neighbouring** forests and **fields**.

9. The police said that the **thief** had probably entered the apartment **quietly** from the **nieghbour's** balcony.

10. Our **friends**, who had been so worried, gave a great sigh of **relief** when they **recieved** the good news.

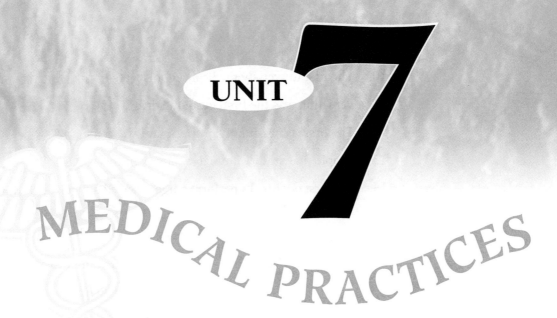

MEDICAL PRACTICES

WHEN DID IT START?

People have been practising medicine since ancient times. At one time, people used herbs and plants to heal themselves. Gradually, they learned more about the human body, and drugs and surgeries were used as well. What do you know about medical practices throughout the ages?

  A Read these statements with a partner and decide whether they are true or false.

1. Surgery was invented in the nineteeth century.

2. Radium was first used to take X-rays.

3. Florence Nightingale introduced modern nursing methods.

4. Vitamins were discovered in the early 1900s.

5. The first transplant of an artificial heart took place in the 1970s.

6. Pacemakers are used for people with blocked arteries.

7. The first vaccination was for polio.

8. Freud developed the psychoanalytic method of treating mental illness.

9. X-rays and radium were first used to diagnose and treat cancer in the 1890s.

10.   The first university medical schools were in the United States.

11.   Penicillin was the first antibiotic drug.

12.   The first successful organ transplant was a liver.

13.   People first studied human anatomy in the 1800s.

14.   The first doctors to perform surgery sewed a piece of cloth to the patient's skin.

15.   Hippocrates raised medicine to the scientific level.

16.   The ancient Egyptians had a system for treating disease.

17.   Anesthesia was first used in the twentieth century.

18.   Cryosurgery uses extreme heat during surgery.

B   Consult the time line on the bottom of pages 90–93 to check your answers.

MEDICINE AROUND THE WORLD

 Choose the best words to complete the paragraphs.

People (**1.** have, is, get) sick all over the world, but treatment (**2.** for, by, since) different medical conditions can vary greatly from one culture to (**3.** other, another, others). For example, in traditional Chinese medicine, a doctor will take your (**4.** breath, weight, pulse) at different points on or near both wrists. So a Chinese patient visiting a doctor in North America may (**5.** worry, wonder, hope) that the doctor is not doing an adequate (**6.** job, surgery, help) when the pulse is taken in only one spot.

Time Line

The ancient Egyptians developed a system for treating disease.

The first university medical schools developed in Europe.

| PRE-HISTORIC TIMES | 2500 BC | c. 400 BC | 1100s | 1500s |

People used the first known surgical treatment—cutting holes in the skull to release evil spirits.

Ancient Greek physicians, led by Hippocrates, raised medicine to a scientific level.

People first studied human anatomy.

In countries such (**7.** like, if, as) Vietnam and China, diet is very (**8.** used, important, strange) in managing health and preventing disease. Yet North Americans have different views on what makes a good (**9.** meal, diet, food). Doctors in North America may only discuss diet if you have an allergy, or if you are (**10.** nervous, overweight, hungry).

Some patients use herbal medicines, which can be very powerful. (**11.** Always, Never, Sometimes) patients neglect to tell (**12.** their, your, our) doctors about herbal remedies they are taking, and may be (**13.** give, gave, given) a drug that conflicts with, or is too strong to (**14.** take, eat, help) with their herbal remedies.

In the Middle East, India, and Africa, antibiotics are available without (**15.** order, prescription, package), and people may take a very casual approach towards using (**16.** its, them, lots). People do not always take the antibiotics as long as they should, and sometimes (**17.** eat, take, share) them with other family members who show similar symptoms.

MEDICINE: IT'S NOT ALL THE SAME

A Scan the text. What is it about?

1. an explanation of the superiority of western medicine

2. a comparison of medical practices in different cultures

3. a description of alternative medicine treatments

The first vaccination was given, for smallpox. This led to the development of vaccines for other diseases.

Florence Nightingale introduced modern nursing methods.

Mid-1500s   **1796**   **1846**   **Mid-1800s**

Doctors started to use surgery. They would sew pieces of cloth that had been glued to the patient's skin.

Anesthesia for surgery was first used.

Medicine: It's Not All the Same

Andrew Weil, M.D.

Most of us would like to think that Western medical practice is based on an unvarying scientific standard. But conventional medicine varies significantly from culture to culture.

Science writer Lynn Payer compared the practice of medicine in West Germany, France, England and the United States, and found that if you went to doctors in each of these countries with the same set of symptoms, you'd likely receive four different treatments, and maybe even different diagnoses. A patient with fatigue and dizziness, for example, might be given a liver tonic by a French doctor, while a German doctor would likely prescribe heart medicine, an American treat for a virus, and an English doctor do nothing at all. The basic medical philosophies underlying the practice in each country vary as well. Whereas the English and Americans tend to view illness as caused by an outside invader, the French and Germans are more likely to blame a weakness in the body's ability to heal. Here are some of Payer's observations about each culture.

France: Poor health is seen by the French as a breakdown in the integrity of the body's terrain (literally, "landscape" or "field"), perhaps a metaphorical way of describing natural resistance. Doctors in France tend to emphasize preventative medicine, and are more likely to prescribe one of the "gentle therapies"—vitamins, tonics, a visit to a spa—than a dose of antibiotics. The French use less aggressive drugs than do Americans, and in smaller doses, and they perform fewer and more limited operations. Because aesthetic concerns are valued, the usual treatment for breast cancer is radiation rather than disfiguring surgery. Aromatherapy, the medical use of fragrant essential oils, is well respected.

One French idiosyncrasy is the belief that liver dysfunction, not germs or viruses, is the frequent cause of ill health—everything from migraines to acne to hay fever.

Germany: In Germany, the heart is supreme. Although the death rate from heart disease in Germany is no greater than in France or Britain, six times more heart drugs are sold there. Poor circulation is blamed for a wide variety of ailments, and German doctors are so enthusiastic about circulatory insufficiency as a diagnosis that they commonly prescribe drugs to raise low blood pressure—a condition not considered pathological in North America. They also routinely prescribe digitalis to anyone over 60 whether the person has symptoms or not.

X-rays were discovered and used to diagnose disease and treat cancer.

Freud developed the psychoanalytic method of treating people with mental illness.

1865   **1895**   **1898**   **c. 1900**   **Early 1900s**

Antiseptic surgery was introduced. A spray of carbolic acid was used on surgical wounds to prevent infection.

Marie and Pierre Curie discovered radium, widely used for treating cancer.

The existence of vitamins was demonstrated.

The German belief in nature as healer leads to a reliance on alternative healing methods such as homeopathy and herbal medicine. German doctors prefer to work with the natural forces of the body to bring about health, and their health insurance system allows for longer cures. There were no antibiotics on a recently published list of the 20 most prescribed drugs in Germany.

England: The most striking characteristic of British medicine is its economy—British doctors do less of nearly everything. Whether this is due to the classic British stiff upper lip or the vagaries of the National Health System, studies show that the British do fewer medical tests, spend less time with patients, prescribe fewer drugs, do less surgery, and express less interest in vitamins or tonics to build up resistance. British doctors always seem to consider the question, Is this treatment better than doing nothing? Often enough, the answer is no.

United States: Americans, of course, favour action—any action—to fight off the foreign elements invading our bodies. American doctors do more diagnostic testing than their counterparts and often prefer surgery over drug therapy. When they do prescribe drugs, they choose stronger ones and use them in higher doses. American doctors are also more likely to overestimate the danger of doing nothing and underestimate the risks of treatment—and this may account for higher rates of physician-caused illness. In Payer's belief, the aggressiveness of American medicine may mirror a history of heroic action, frontier mentality, and can-do attitude.

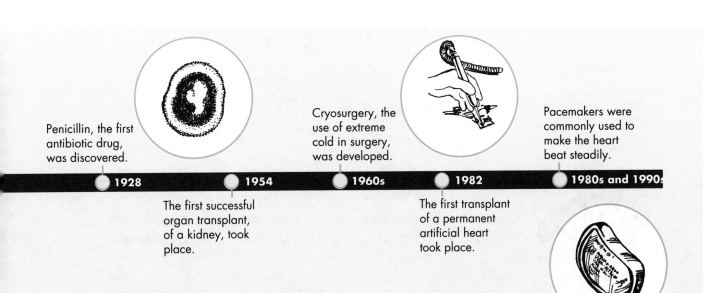

Penicillin, the first antibiotic drug, was discovered.

Cryosurgery, the use of extreme cold in surgery, was developed.

Pacemakers were commonly used to make the heart beat steadily.

1928   1954   1960s   1982   1980s and 1990s

The first successful organ transplant, of a kidney, took place.

The first transplant of a permanent artificial heart took place.

B   Read the text again. Write the correct country or countries for each statement about medical practices.

Which country or countries:

> sell six times more heart drugs than other countries.   **Germany**

1. do less of almost everything

2. believe liver problems cause ill health

3. favour surgery to drugs

4. view illness as an outside invader

5. favour action

6. use higher doses of drugs

7. rely on alternative healing methods

8. favour gentle therapies such as tonics and vitamins

9. had no antibiotics on the list of 20 most prescribed drugs

10. have higher rates of doctor-induced illness

11. value aesthetic concerns

12. commonly treat patients for low blood pressure

13. see poor health as a breakdown of the body's terrain

14. believe many illnesses stem from the heart and poor circulation

15. question whether treatment is better than doing nothing

16. underestimate the risks of treatment

CANADIAN CAPSULES   Medic-Alert bracelets and medallions are worn by many Canadians. They are used to alert medical personnel to pre-existing medical conditions.

DIFFERENT CUSTOMS

Getting sick can be frightening, and it's worse if you are in a new culture with medical treatments that are different from the ones you are used to.

A   Discuss these questions in a group.

1.   Have you been to a doctor's office here?

2.   Have you been to a hospital clinic here?

3.   Have you stayed in a hospital here?

4.   Have you had medical treatment in any other country?

5.   What similarities or differences did you notice?

B   Which of these medical practices would you expect a doctor to perform, if you went for diagnosis of a problem?

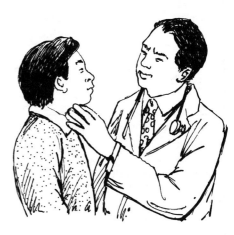

1.   do a complete examination

2.   send you for tests

3.   take your pulse on your wrist

4.   take your pulse in several different points

5.   take your blood pressure

6.   examine your tongue

7.   take your medical history

8.   spend a long time with you

9.   spend only a few minutes with you

10.   prescribe a drug

11.   take a "wait and see" attitude

12.   prescribe an over-the-counter medicine

13.   suggest an alternative therapy (acupuncture, homeopathy, herbs)

14.   suggest surgery

15.   refer you to a specialist

16.   suggest vitamins or tonics

17.   suggest a change in diet or lifestyle

18.   other (Explain.)

C If you had the problems or conditions listed below, what would you expect a doctor to do:

a) in Canada

b) in another country that you know

Complete the chart.

Problems	In Canada	Elsewhere
You have a cold and a cough.		
You have a rash on your arms.		
You have an earache.		
You feel tired and dizzy.		
Your blood pressure is high.		
Your blood pressure is low.		
You have trouble sleeping at night.		
You feel very nervous.		
You think you have an allergy.		
You have an upset stomach.		
You have gained, or lost, a lot of weight.		
You have a backache.		

CANADIAN CAPSULES Every day in Canada, doctors write over 500 000 prescriptions for antibiotics. The most commonly prescribed antibiotic is Ampicillin.

 **Passive Voice**

When the **active voice** is used, the subject is the agent (doer) of the action. If the sentence contains an object, it is the recipient of the action.

The child broke her arm.		
s	v	o
agent	active form	recipient

When the **passive voice** is used, the subject is the recipient of the action. The agent or doer (mentioned or understood) is the object of the sentence.

The medical form was destroyed accidentally.		(by the secretary)
s	v	(o)
recipient	passive form	(agent)

The passive voice is more common in writing than in speaking. News reports and text books often contain examples of the passive voice to focus on the event or process rather than the agent or doer.

The passive form of the verb requires the auxiliary verb **be** + the past participle of the main verb. The auxiliary verb **be** shows time (past, present, future).

> The instructions **are written** on the package.
> The X-ray **was taken** in the emergency ward.
> The cast **will be removed** in six weeks.

  A Do the quiz below, noting the use of the passive verb form as you answer the questions.

1. How many litres of blood are contained in the human body?
   a) 6
   b) 12
   c) 25

2. The sense that is least developed in human beings is
   a) smell
   b) hearing
   c) taste

3. Children are cared for by
   a) pediatricians
   b) orthopedists
   c) gerontologists

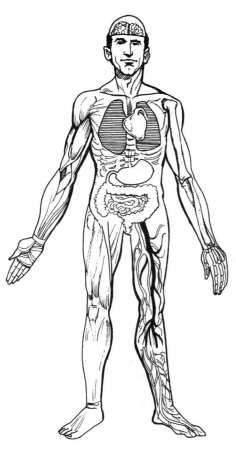

4. The skin is replaced
    a) once a year
    b) every few months
    c) every few weeks

5. The central nervous system is made up of
    a) the brain and nerves
    b) the heart and lungs
    c) the eyes and ears

6. How many bones are found in the human body?
    a) 175
    b) 206
    c) 359

7. Blood is called
    a) the river of life
    b) the staff of life
    c) the water of life

8. More than a third of the body's weight is composed of
    a) muscle
    b) skin
    c) bones

9. Our food is processed by the
    a) liver
    b) digestive system
    c) stomach

10. Sixty-six percent to the body is made up of
    a) bones
    b) water
    c) blood

B   Give the passive form of the verbs. Use the tense indicated in brackets.

> we see (future) **we will be seen**

1. we examine (past)
2. you call (future)
3. he tells (past)
4. you meet (present)
5. it removes (future)
6. you hurt (past)
7. his instructions follow (future)
8. you give (past)
9. he asks (past)
10. it protects (present)

C Change the sentences to the passive voice. **Omit the doer**.

> The doctor gave a prescription to the patient.
> **The patient was given a prescription.**

1. The herbalist collected the herbs in the forest.

2. The doctor will see the patient in a few minutes.

3. A technician will remove the cast next Tuesday.

4. The technician took several X-rays of his leg.

5. The doctor checked my pulse and temperature.

6. The pharmacist usually writes the instructions on the bottle.

7. They put the injured man on a stretcher immediately.

8. A pharmacist fills prescriptions according to the doctor's instructions.

9. Doctors found acupuncture to be effective in his case.

10. The doctor ordered complete bed rest to cure the flu.

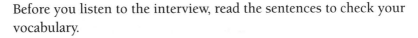
EVALUATING ALTERNATIVE MEDICINE

CBC

 LISTENING ACTIVITY *7* *Interview with Dr. Joseph Jacobs*

  A Before you listen to the interview, read the sentences to check your vocabulary.

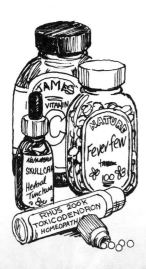

1. The Office of Alternative Medicine wants to evaluate the scientific validity of alternative medical practices.

2. The program will focus on one specific treatment.

3. Homeopathic medicine uses large amounts of diluted products.

4. Some people feel this medicine doesn't really work.

5. There are many medications to which people respond, although doctors don't understand why.

6. The scientific community uses clinical trials to test the effectiveness of medications.

7. Dr. Jacobs has an open mind about alternative therapies.

8. There is a lot of anecdotal evidence that homeopathy works.

9. Not many doctors in Canada practise homeopathy.

10. Many people worry that alternative medicine is part of a trend to reject science.

11. Dr. Jacobs agrees that alternative medicine compromises science.

12. Dr. Jacob's mother used herbal remedies.

13. Herbal remedies are based on thousands of years of trial and error.

14. Dr. Jacobs believes some of the herbal remedies are quite effective.

 B Listen and write **T** (true) or **F** (false) for the statements in Exercise A. Use the worksheet.

IN MY OPINION

If You Are Sick

 Different cultures have different ideas about the role of a doctor. Discuss what you think should be done in the following cases.

1. You are in the emergency ward of the hospital because you have severe pains in your stomach. You are alone and the doctor assigned to examine you is an intern of the opposite sex. You don't think you would feel comfortable discussing your symptoms with him or her. Would it be appropriate to ask to be seen by another doctor who is on duty?

2. Your doctor has examined you, done tests, and recommended a treatment for a medical problem you have. You understand the doctor's instructions but you don't really understand what is wrong with you and what the treatment is all about. Would you ask for an explanation or would you simply trust the doctor's training and experience?

3. Your aunt has been sick for some time and has undergone a lot of tests to find out what is wrong with her. Her doctor has seen the test results and feels that the patient has a disease that will probably be fatal. Your aunt is an emotional person and the doctor isn't sure whether to tell her the real diagnosis or simply to treat her symptoms and try to make her comfortable. What would you advise?

4. You have been having a medical problem that isn't life-threatening but that is unpleasant and sometimes painful. Your doctor has recommended that you have surgery to correct the problem. However, the doctor admits that the surgical procedure isn't effective in 100 percent of cases and that you may still have the same problem after surgery. You aren't sure if the surgery is a good idea. Would you seek a second opinion?

5. You go to the doctor for a routine check-up and the doctor finds you have a problem and suggests that you see a specialist. Your friend has a similar problem and his doctor told him to go to a physiotherapist for treatment. He feels much better. Would you follow your doctor's advice, tell your doctor about your friend, ask your friend for the name of his physiotherapist and say nothing to your doctor, or get another opinion?

What Do You Expect?

 What are your expectations of the medical system? Use the ideas from the unit to write about what you expect when you visit the doctor. Which practices make you feel comfortable? Which situations make you feel uncomfortable? How does the medical system in Canada compare with other systems you have experienced?

SHARPEN YOUR ENGLISH

Vocabulary

 Match the doctor with the specialty.

Doctor Directory

1. ophthalmologist		a)	skin problems
2. orthodontist		b)	heart problems
3. obstetrician		c)	blood diseases
4. podiatrist		d)	cancer
5. urologist		e)	pregnancy
6. pediatrician		f)	brain disorders
7. gynecologist		g)	problems of the elderly
8. oncologist		h)	eye diseases
9. dermatologist		i)	foot problems
10. neurologist		j)	bones and muscles
11. endocrinologist		k)	X-rays
12. cardiologist		l)	children's problems
13. hematologist		m)	women's problems
14. orthopedist		n)	urinary and kidney problems
15. gerontologist		o)	problems with glands
16. radiologist		p)	the teeth

Pronunciation

Pronounce the names of the specialists with your teacher and mark the primary stress. Then practise with a partner to say the words correctly.

UNIT 8

PASSAGES

THE BEST TIME

A Work together. Describe what you see in the pictures. How old do you think the people in the pictures are?

B   Talk about what would be a good time in life to do each of the things listed below. Use the worksheet.

Ages:	0–12 Child	13–17 Teen	18–25 Young adult	25–40 Adult	40–60 Middle aged	60+ Retired
learn to drive a car						
graduate from college						
retire (stop working)						
have a child						
get your first job						
travel around the world						
make life-long friends						
go to the doctor alone						
expect a promotion at work						
get married						
start dating						
become a grandparent						
leave home						
buy a house						
take a sabbatical						
get a serious job						
get a driver's licence						
get your own apartment						
study in another city						
cross the street alone						
have a steady boyfriend or girlfriend						
go on vacation with a friend						
vote in an election						
have a part-time job						
buy your first car						
start saving money for retirement						
choose your own clothes						
have a summer job						
stop depending on your parents for money						
work as a volunteer						

CBC  *VIDEO ACTIVITY* 4

A Discuss these questions in groups.

1. Where do people usually find mates in Canada?

2. Where did you, your parents, or any couples you know meet their mates?

3. What kind of social activities are available to young couples in the city?

4. What kind of social activities do young couples who live in the country enjoy?

5. What problems do you think young men and women could encounter in finding a mate if they live in the country?

B Read the questions with a partner. Then watch the video and answer the questions.

1. Where does the story take place?

2. What kind of background do people want their dates to have?

3. How old is Lana?

4. What kind of man is Lana looking for?

5. What problem does she have when she dates men from the city?

6. Why is Lana lonely in winter?

7. How far apart do neighbours live?

8. What is "Country Introductions"?

9. How many people are signed up?

10. What are they looking for?

11. Why do marriages between city women and farmers frequently end in divorce?

12. What does Sheryl guarantee her customers, and for what price?

13. What attracted Diane to Jim?

14. Why didn't Jim's previous relationships start off well?

15. What does Diane say about their relationship?

16. What does Lana hope to share with someone?

FINDING A MATE

Discuss these questions in a group.

1. Would the problem in the video come up in other cultures you know about?

2. How important do you think common interests should be when choosing a mate?

3. Would you be willing to change your lifestyle radically if you really loved someone and wanted to be married?

4. Choose the things that are most important to you in a marriage partner. Put them in order. Number 1 is most important.

   intelligence   personality
   good looks   occupation
   common interests   temperament
   money   religion

5. Write about what is important to you in a mate. Which things are most important to you? What would you be willing to change if you really loved someone? What would you not be willing to change?

The term "rites of passage" was invented by a French anthropologist. He used the term to describe the common purpose of ceremonies such as graduations and weddings.

RITES OF PASSAGE

  A Choose the best words to complete the paragraphs.

**passage anniversary food major child graduation entry
dressing another ceremonies adulthood transitions**

In all cultures we have rituals to mark the __1_____ events in our
lives. An occasion such as the birth of a __2_____, the loss of
baby teeth, __3_____ from school, getting married, or reaching a
certain __4_____ calls for ceremonies and celebrations. The
occasions and the __5_____ may vary from one culture to
another, but they all mark transitions. These __6_____ and the
ceremonies that mark them are called rites of passage.

Rites of __7_____ are shared with family and friends and
generally involve special ways of __8_____, solemn ceremonies,
and the sharing of festive meals. The particular customs and
__9_____ will vary from one occasion to another and from one
culture to __10_____. But the underlying idea is the same—the rite
of passage signals the __11_____ into a new role for the celebrant.
One of the most widespread customs is the celebration reaching
__12_____, but other passages are also common to many cultures.

  B Look at the pictures of Canadians. What events are being celebrated?

  C Discuss some ceremonies that are particular to **your** culture. Explain the
customs that surround them to your group.

D Write about a ceremony in your culture. What does it mean to you?

Tag Questions

A tag question is a short expression that is used at the end of a sentence for one of two reasons: to seek confirmation or agreement, or to ask for information.

1. Use a tag question when you already know the answer and are asking the other person to confirm your opinion. How you phrase the question anticipates the answer you expect.

> It's a beautiful day, isn't it? (The answer expected is, "Yes it is.")
>
> It isn't too hard, is it? (The answer expected is, "No it isn't.")

Note: The question tag has falling intonation in questions of confirmation.

> We aren't late, are we?

2. Use a tag question to ask a question to which you don't know the answer.

> You haven't paid the bill, have you?
>
> Possible answers: Yes, I have. No, I haven't.

Note: The question tag when you want information has rising intonation.

> He is our old teacher from high school, isn't he?

A Match the statements with the tag questions.

1.	Paul Malley was always nice,	a) wasn't she?
2.	You aren't going to the school reunion,	b) aren't I?
3.	Sue Mills is an excellent mother,	c) were we?
4.	The invitation is beautifully engraved,	d) isn't she?
5.	The cruise brochures are interesting,	e) weren't you?
6.	I'm the oldest person at the table,	f) wasn't he?
7.	He wasn't her first boyfriend,	g) was he?
8.	She was the best swimmer,	h) are you?
9.	You were in our graduating class,	i) isn't it?
10.	We weren't supposed to dress formally,	j) aren't they?

B   Write tag questions for these sentences.

1. Michel Lacroix teaches at a large college,

2. Max didn't forget to lock the door to the apartment,

3. You all enjoy playing a game of ping-pong,

4. Children these days like to play electronic games,

5. Your friends went to a movie last night,

6. Canadians don't mind going out in cold weather,

7. We ate later than usual yesterday evening,

8. High school graduation is a big occasion,

9. They weren't married at City Hall,

10. That couple met at a hockey game,

THE STRESS OF CHANGE

A   Read this paragraph. Then close your book and write as the teacher dictates.

> We often think of stress as something bad. Some stress is harmful and may lead us towards heart attacks and other health problems. However, without stress we probably wouldn't get up in the morning or accomplish much in life either. Scientists tell us that stress is caused by both bad and good things that happen in our lives. One of the great causes of stress is change itself, so many of life's transitions are stressful.

B   Work in a group to discuss these questions.

1. What are some major events in a person's life that can cause stress?

2. Why can getting married be stressful?

3. Why is moving to a new house usually a stressful activity?

4. Is starting a new job stressful even if you like the job? Why?

5. What is the most stressful experience you have had recently?

6. Do you think of any of these activities as stressful? Explain your answer.

    a) vacations   d) going back to school

    b) being sick   e) getting a promotion at work

    c) buying a car   f) redecorating your living room

TAKE THE STRESS TEST

The Holmes-Rahe Test measures the impact of life changes on our stress levels. The higher your score, the greater your risk of accidents and illness.

Look at the list and choose the life changes you have experienced **in the last year**. Then add up your score.

Death of a spouse 100

Divorce 73

Marital separation 65

Detention in jail 63

Death of a close family member 63

Major personal injury or illness 53

Marriage 50

Being fired at work 47

Marital reconciliation 45

Retirement from work 45

Major change in your health or the health of a family member 44

Pregnancy 40

Gaining a new family member through birth, adoption, or marriage 39

Major business readjustments 39

Major changes in financial state 38

Death of a close friend 37

Change to a different line of work 36

Major increase in the number of arguments with spouse 35

Taking on a mortgage 31

Promotion, demotion, or transfer at work 29

Son or daughter leaving home 29

In-law troubles 29

Outstanding personal achievement 28

Going back to school 26

Moving or major redecorating 25

Revision of personal habits 24

Trouble with supervisor at work 23

Major change in work hours 20

Changes in residence 20

Change to a new school 20

Major change in type or amount of recreation 19

Major change in church activities 19

Major change in social activities 18

Buying a car 17

Major changes in sleeping habits 16

Major changes in number of family get-togethers 15

Vacation 13

Holiday observances 12

Traffic tickets 11

The risk of accident or illness within 2 years is calculated on the following basis:

300 + = 80 percent

150 – 300 = 51 percent

35 – 150 = 35 percent

In Canada, the average age of a person getting married for the first time is 25 for a woman and 27 for a man.

A These are some expression from the story that follows. Match the expressions to the words.

1. a black-tie dinner   a) action

2. struggled to fasten   b) difficulty

3. The hair on the back of my neck rose.   c) upset

4. break the news   d) reciprocate

5. I swung into automatic pilot.   e) speed

6. in a flash   f) communicate

7. to burst into tears   g) formality

8. to return the favour   h) fear

B Skim the story to answer these questions.

1. What happened to Dani's mother?

2. When did Dani first feel that her and her mother's roles were reversed?

3. Why was Dani worried about the future?

Suddenly Grown-up

Dani Shapiro

It was five o'clock on a weekday, and I had finished work early in order to prepare for the evening ahead, a black-tie dinner. At the moment the phone rang, I was getting dressed for the party. I struggled to fasten an earring while I let the answering machine pick up.

"Hello? Hello, is anybody there?" an unfamiliar woman's voice asked. "I'm looking for Dani Shapiro—could somebody please pick up the phone? Hello?" She sounded vaguely hysterical.

I grabbed the phone. "I'm here." I was not yet frightened. "How can I help you?" She paused, and in that pause the hair on the back of my neck began to rise.

"Dani, I don't want to upset you, but there's been an accident," she said. "Your mother was in the back of a cab that was hit by a car. She's been taken by ambulance to the hospital."

I don't want to upset you. The words were terrifyingly familiar. Nine years earlier, when I was 23, my father was killed in a car crash. I was living across the country at the time, and when my aunt called to break the news to me, she, too, paused and told me she didn't want to upset me. As if, in the breath she drew before giving me information that would forever change my life, she were trying to offer me a final moment of consolation. As if I had one last second to still be a child.

A strange calm seeped into my body and I swung into automatic pilot. Wallet, purse, house keys—out the door in a flash. I ran downstairs and took a taxi to the hospital. As I dashed through the swinging doors of the emergency room I saw my mother sitting on a plastic chair in the waiting room with an ice pack to her head, a bump the size of a small egg swelling above one eyebrow. She looked at me, eyes wide as a toddler's, and burst into tears.

In the examining room, an emergency-room physician (who looked younger than I) peered into her eyes with a pinpoint light and tried to calm her shivers. Then he turned toward me: "How old is your mother? Does she have any allergies? Has she ever had surgery? A heart condition?" It occurred to me that this must be at least as odd for my mother as for me; now our roles were reversed and I was answering for her. I felt the full weight of adulthood flutter above my shoulders and settle there, perhaps permanently.

Beneath the fluorescent glare of the emergency-room lights, my mother smiled weakly at me. The skin around her eyes was already starting to turn black-and-blue, but the doctor told her that it wasn't serious. She was going to be all right.

"Look at my daughter," she beamed at the doctor. "Isn't she beautiful?" He turned obligingly toward my evening dress, carefully chosen for a dinner-dance but utterly absurd in this situation. Suddenly I felt like I was my mother's child once more.

As I looked at her, I realized that even though she was OK this time, I was getting my first glimpse of the future that we will inevitably share, no doubt in hospitals just like this. Once it was I who turned to her, frightened and needy, hoping she would guide me into adulthood. Now it was my chance to return the favour. But how? Where am I guiding my mother? Certainly no place I have been before.

I remember the way she took care of her own mother before she died a few years ago at the age of 94. When I accompanied my mother to the nursing home where my grandmother lived out her last days, I would listen to my mother's cheerful voice, and buried beneath it I would hear her own neediness, a desire for mothering that never seems to go away.

When my grandmother grew unresponsive, my mother would smile and stroke her hand, as I now was stroking my mother's hand. "Is everything going to be OK?" my mother asked me shakily. I know there is more than one answer to this question. Everything is fine for now, but I couldn't help thinking five years—or ten, or 20—down the line. When I was a child, I would ask my mother for answers, and believe she had them. But none of us has answers. We just pretend we do. We have no knowledge to pass along, only comfort. As the responsibility for each other shifts between generations, so must the willingness to bear the burden of pretending. And so, I find the strength inside myself. Yes, mother. Everything's going to be all right.

  C Read the story again and answer the questions.

1. What was Dani doing when the phone rang?

2. Why were the words on the telephone "terrifyingly familiar" to Dani?

3. What did Dani feel about the reason the woman said "I don't want to upset you"?

4. What did Dani's mother do when she saw Dani?

5. What kind of questions did the doctor ask Dani about her mother?

6. Why does Dani say "I felt the full weight of adulthood flutter above my shoulders and settle there, perhaps permanently?"

7. What made Dani feel like a child again?

8.   What kind of future did she see for herself and her mother?

9.   What two opposite things did Dani hear in her mother's voice at the nursing home?

10.   What does Dani mean by the "burden of pretending"?

BECOMING AN ADULT

 LISTENING ACTIVITY 8

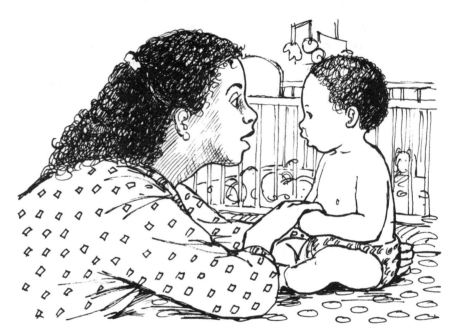

A   Discuss these questions in a group.

1.   Do you feel like an adult?

2.   Do you think that there is a precise moment when someone becomes an adult?

3.   Which characteristics do you think define an adult?

4.   Which characteristics that defined an adult in the past are different today?

5.   What are some privileges that adults have but children don't?

6.   What are some advantages of being a child?

B   Listen and answer the questions. Use the worksheet.

1.   What did Deborah realize when she was unhappy about staying in the hospital?

2.   What was the turning point for Deborah?

3.   What happened to Steve when he was working in a store last summer?

4.   What other two events made him feel like a grown-up?

5.   Give some information about Tara.

6.   What does Tara think will make her feel like an adult?

7.   Give some information about Chuck.

8.   What did Chuck think about the doctors who treated his son?

9.   Over the years, how did his ideas about doctors change?

10. What made Chuck feel like an adult, when he was having dinner with his family at the restaurant?

11. What does the interviewer sometimes say to her children?

12. What does she say about how we become adults?

IN MY OPINION

What Is an Adult?

A   These comments were made by a group of young people who were asked to define the meaning of "adult," and to say whether they were adults themselves. With which statements do you agree?

Questions: What is an adult? Are you one?

1.   Well, legally yes, because I turned 18 in May.

2.   An adult is someone who works and doesn't need the financial support of his or her parents.

3.   Being an adult is an attitude you should assume when you are ready for it.

4.   I will get there one day by mastering my thoughts and discovering who I am.

5.   For me, being an adult is not a question of age because some people are old but still act like 10 year olds.

6. Being an adult is when you can live on your own without asking anyone how to live your life.

7. I think we should include the word "responsibility" when we talk about being an adult.

8. I consider that I'm an adult because I'm not living with my parents anymore.

9. They label us adults at the age of 18, but I think that's wrong.

10. You are an adult when you can stop thinking only of yourself and think of others too.

11. Adults have more freedom to do what they want.

12. Adults get more respect than children do.

13. I think that a lot of so-called adults act like children.

14. I personally think that an adult knows when he or she is one. Adults probably don't know when they got there but the number of bills reminds them.

15. I'm an adult because I'm able to have a conversation with someone much older than me without getting bored.

16. An adult is old, has a lot of responsibilities, is working, is living by himself or herself, and is serious.

17. You don't do stupid things anymore.

18. The job thing is really important, because you're not responsible if you don't deal with money.

    B Add two or three statements of your own. Discuss them with your group.

 C Write your ideas about becoming an adult.

CANADIAN CAPSULES People often pass through rites of passage in groups. For example, students graduating from high school or college sit together in special areas separated from their parents. They also wear special clothing, such as black gowns and caps, to symbolize their transition.

SHARPEN YOUR ENGLISH

What Do You Say?

Work in a group. Discuss the correct thing to say in each of the circumstances.

1. A friend mentions that it is her birthday.

   a) "How old are you?"

   b) "Congratulations!"

   c) "Many happy returns."

2. You learn that a female friend is engaged to be married.

   a) "Best wishes."

   b) "Many happy returns."

   c) "I can't believe it."

3. You hear that a friend's grandfather has died.

   a) "What happened to him?"

   b) "Oh well. He was pretty old anyway."

   c) "Please accept my condolences."

4.   A neighbour is going into the hospital for an operation.

a)   "What is the matter with you?"

b)   "I'm sorry. I hope it's not too serious."

c)   "Are you sure you have a good doctor?"

5.   Your friend has just left the hospital after surgery for a serious illness.

a)   "I hope you don't need to have another operation."

b)   "Congratulations on surviving the surgery."

c)   "I'm glad to see you looking so much better."

6.   You have been invited to the wedding of some friends of a different religion and aren't sure what their customs are.

a)   "Are there any particular customs I should know about?"

b)   "I hope you don't expect me to wear some strange costume."

c)   "You aren't going to expect me to eat some weird food, are you?"

7.   A neighbour with four girls tells you that she is expecting another baby.

a)   "Well, I sure hope you manage to have a boy this time."

b)   "Congratulations. You must both be very excited."

c)   "Was this new baby planned or was it an accident?"

8.   Your friend from the office tells you he is engaged to be married.

a)   "You're kidding. Who are you going to marry?

b)   "Congratulations! When is the wedding going to be?"

c)   "I hope your marriage works out OK."

9.   You have friends who are getting divorced and you are talking to one member of the couple.

a)   "Well, I'm not surprised. We never really liked your spouse anyway."

b)   "I'm sorry to hear this news. It must be a painful experience for you both."

c)   "I don't believe in divorce. Shouldn't you try to stay together for the children?"

10.   Your neighbour just lost his job because his company downsized.

a)   "Oh, how terrible. How are you going to get another job at your age?"

b)   "Well, at least you weren't the only one the company let go."

c)   "Sorry to hear it. I'm sure you won't be on the job market long."

BUY ME! BUY ME!

HOW I CHOOSE

Work in a group. Look at the products below and discuss what you consider when you buy these things. Use the factors listed to help you.

Products

1. a television
2. a watch
3. a jacket
4. shampoo
5. sneakers
6. a car
7. laundry detergent
8. a chocolate bar
9. deodorant
10. ketchup
11. a couch
12. coffee or tea
13. a can of soup
14. jeans
15. a toaster

Factors to consider

price	effectiveness
quality	ease of use
design	guarantee
taste	safety
comfort	brand name
endurance	nutritional value

119

SEDUCED IN THE SUPERMARKET

  A Look at the products below. Which brand names do you know for these products?

  B Read the sentences below with a partner. Answer true or false.

1. Packages and containers are carefully tested before they reach supermarket shelves.

2. In the supermarket, people generally choose products based on their contents, rather than on price or packaging.

3. People often have a hard time distinguishing between a product and its package.

4. Some companies develop the package before the product.

5. Size and shape are the most important part of packaging.

6. People often choose products for subjective reasons.

7. People often buy products because they feel lonely or anxious.

Read the article quickly. Compare your answers to Exercise B with the information in the text.

Seduced in the Supermarket

Thomas Hine

1. During a typical 30-minute shopping trip down the aisles of an average supermarket, tens of thousands of products vie for your attention. Ultimately, many will make you believe they are worth a try. How? Packaging—the silent but nevertheless persuasive salesman.

2. Each box and jar, stand-up pouch and squeeze bottle, each can, bag, tube and sprayer has been carefully designed to speak to your inner self. Are you a good parent, a good provider? Do you care about the environment? Do you appreciate the finer things in life? Wouldn't you really like something chocolate?

3. Each detail has been carefully considered, reworked and tested in samples on store shelves. Refinements are measured in millimetres, for the designers want you to see far more than a container and a label. You are buying a personality, an attitude, perhaps even a set of beliefs.

4. A pioneer in studying people's emotional response to packages was Louis Cheskin, a specialist in the psychology of marketing who began his research in the 1930s. He placed identical products in two different packages, one with circles, the other with triangles. Then he asked his subjects which product they preferred, and why. Over 80 percent chose the product in the box with the circles. They believed the contents would be of higher quality.

5. "I had difficulty believing the results after the first 200 interviews," Cheskin wrote later. "But after 1000 interviews, I had to accept the fact that the majority of consumers transferred the sensation from the container to its contents." And there was another surprise: Even after trying these identical products, people overwhelmingly preferred those in the package with the circles.

6. Cheskin repeated the experiments for a wide variety of product types. He found, for instance, that the look of the package has an enormous impact on how crackers taste or how soaps are perceived to clean.

7. Cheskin named this phenomenon "sensation transference." It became the foundation not only of his career as a consultant to companies like Procter & Gamble and McDonald's, but of much of the research in package design done since.

8. One of the most dramatic versions of the Cheskin experiment involved an underarm deodorant mailed in packages with three different colour schemes to a test group. The group was told that three different formulations were under consideration, and was asked to judge them.

9. Results: Colour scheme B was considered just right. Scheme C was said to be strong smelling but not very effective. And Scheme A was deemed downright threatening. Several participants developed skin rashes after using it and had to consult dermatologists. Yet all three deodorants were exactly the same!

10. As Walter Stern notes in a prominent textbook on the subject: "Consumers generally do not distinguish between a product and its package. Many products are packages—and many packages are products. One leading package design firm, Primo Angeli of San Francisco, has carried this principle to a money-making extreme: the firm designs packaging for products that do not yet exist. The packaging is then tested and the marketing concept refined. Only when it's clear that the company has a winner on its hands will it need to go to the expense of actually developing the product.

➡

11. Colour is one of the most potent tools in packaging. Studies of eye movement have shown that colour triggers the fastest response of any element of a package. Take, for example, V8 Vegetable Juice. For decades the general arrangement on the V8 label has stayed more or less the same: a horizontal array of tomatoes defined by greenery, and punctuated by vertical celery and carrots. What you might not notice, but will probably feel, is the intensity of the vegetables' colours. V8 vegetables are not printed with the standard four-colour process used in books and magazines, but with five colours. This lets some of them take on strikingly vivid hue. Thus, the vegetables are mysteriously compelling.

12. There is no doubt that people have strong responses to colours and shapes. But just how these translate into the purchase of a can of soup or a jar of moisturizing cream is not well understood. The process is certainly not rational. "I can't ask you why you like a certain package," says Stan Gross, a marketing consultant based in Haverford, Pa., " And you can't tell me. The package is not silent. It screams—but it screams to your inner mind.

13. Obviously, Gross and the other psychological marketers are dealing with fears and desires that go deeper than whiter laundry. Parents worry that they are failing their children. Individuals feel lonely and unfulfilled. To calm these anxieties through such things as a frozen steak sandwich or a pack of cinnamon chewing gum—-doesn't that sound cruel?

14. Gross argues that people know, on some level, that the purchases they make will not fulfill their deepest wants. "Buying things is a way of coping. They offer compensations for the deficiencies we feel in ourselves " he says. We may know they are empty symbols, but we pursue them because they satisfy us. And perhaps because, at still another level, we enjoy watching their gloriously sophisticated competition for our favours.

  D   Read the article again and find the answer to these questions.

1. Why is packaging called the "silent salesman"?

2. What are some inner feelings the packages are designed to address?

3. What are you really buying when you choose a product?

4. Why did the majority of people choose the product with circles on the box?

5. What was surprising about Cheskin's experiment?

6. What is "sensation transference"?

7. Explain the underarm deodorant experiment.

8. How did the San Francisco firm Primo Angeli exploit the principle that "products are packages"?

9. Explain how colour was used successfully on the V8 vegetable juice container.

10. What kinds of emotions are marketers and psychologists dealing with?

11. Why do people often get pleasure from buying things?

E   Use these clues to find words in the paragraphs. Then use the words to complete the crossword puzzle.

Across

2. convincing, makes you want to do something (paragraph 1)

5. reasonable, sensible (paragraph 12)

7. colour (paragraph 11)

8. something that makes you feel you are in danger (paragraph 9)

11. people who took part in the experiment (paragraph 9)

13. buyers (paragraph 10)

14. powerful, strong (paragraph 11)

15. (a) success (paragraph 10)

Down

1. a period of 10 years (paragraph 11)

3. exactly the same (paragraph 5)

4. worries, fears (paragraph 13)

6. tell the difference between things (paragraph 10)

9. things that are missing (paragraph 14)

10. yells, talks very loudly (paragraph 12)

12. strength, concentration (paragraph 11)

WATCHING YOUR SHOPPING HABITS

LISTENING ACTIVITY 9   *Interview with Eric Hayes,*
Marketing Consultant

 A   Work in a group. Say whether you agree or disagree with the following statements.

1. I like shopping in big stores because everything is easy to find.

2. I like listening to music when I am shopping in a department store.

3. I usually end up buying things I wasn't planning to get when I entered the store.

4. I have had trouble locating the down escalator on the way out.

5. I like the wide variety of choice a department store offers.

6. I like the free samples at the perfume counter in department stores.

7. I would enter a store if I saw something I liked in the window display.

8. I usually go to a department store with a shopping list and stick to it.

9. I prefer shopping with a friend so I can discuss what to buy.

10. I can enter a department store, buy what I need, and leave quickly.

B Read the questions. Then listen and answer. Use the worksheet.

1. What does Eric Hayes do?

2. Why is market research important to department stores?

3. What kind of plans might Eric draw up for a store?

4. What sort of suggestions might he make about layout?

5. Why is it important to display "hot" items in the store window?

6. Why does the store want customers to stay as long as possible?

7. Where is the men's wear located and why?

8. What does Eric mention about the location of the escalators?

9. Why is smell an important marketing tool?

10. What example does Eric give of smell being used for marketing?

11. What are two ways the store can find out what people want to buy?

12. Why are surveys sometimes not reliable?

13. How do spies study people's habits in the department store?

14. What is the interviewer's reaction to the information Eric gives?

Questions With "Like"

There are three types of questions in English that use the word **like**. Each type uses **like** in a different way.

1. **Like** is the main verb and it is used to inquire about personal preference. Put the subject between the auxiliary verb and the main verb.

> What colour do you **like**? I like red.
> Who(m) do you like? I like Annabel.

2. **Like** is used after the main verb **be** and it is used to mean **how something is**. It is used to request information about abstract characteristics such as emotions and atmosphere.

> What is Annabel **like**? She is friendly and curious.

3. **Like** is used in the phrase **looks like** to mean "resemble." It is used to inquire about physical characteristics.

> What (who) does Annabel **look like**? She is tall and has red hair.
> She looks like her sister.

A   Match the questions with the appropriate answers below.

1. What does your new sweater look like?

2. What is The Bay like?

3. What kind of pants do teenagers like?

4. What is West Edmonton Mall like?

5. What does the manager look like?

6. What is the new perfume like?

7. What kind of shoes do you like to wear?

8. What is the new sales clerk like?

9. What does the new soft drink taste like?

10. What does your engagement ring look like?

---

a) sneakers

b) She's tall with blond hair.

c) She's very friendly and helpful.

d) It's huge, with amusement centres and lots of stores.

e) It's a typical department store.

f) like any other cola

g) It's green with a high neck.

h) It's expensive, but it smells wonderful.

i) a small diamond on a gold band

j) blue jeans

B   Make questions that match the answers below. Write questions with **what + like**.

1. Leo is tall with a beard, moustache, and glasses.

2. Mieke is nice and she has a great sense of humour.

3. Steve enjoys listening to jazz and pop music.

4. Charles likes travelling to distant countries.

5. The customer is tall with blond hair.

6. I'm an extremely curious person with many interests.

7. Carolyn absolutely loves to go shopping for shoes.

8. Sales clerks are generally outgoing people.

9. Min Hee is very hardworking. She puts in long hours in the advertising department.

10. The new shopping centre resembles any other suburban mall.

WHAT'S IN A NAME?

 CBC  VIDEO ACTIVITY 5

A Work in a group. Give the brand names of:

1. three kinds of toothpaste
2. three cars that begin with the letter "A" (example: Acura)
3. two different kinds of batteries
4. three kinds of perfume
5. three kinds of shampoo
6. two kinds of watches
7. four kinds of soft drink
8. three kinds of potato chips
9. three brands of sneakers
10. three brands of TV
11. two kinds of cookies
12. three fashion magazines
13. two kinds of coffee
14. three kinds of jeans

CANADIAN CAPSULES

Canadians buy a lot of soup in packages, cans, and cups with instant noodles. A survey showed that, on average, a Canadian household has nine kinds of soup in the kitchen cupboard.

B   Discuss these questions in a group.

1. How often do you choose a product because the name is familiar to you?

2. How often do you buy "no name" or generic products?

3. Do you read advertisements in magazines or newspapers?

4. Do you usually pay attention to TV commercials?

5. How much influence do you think advertisements have on your choice of products?

 C   Watch the video and answer the questions. Use the worksheet.

1. How many different names are registered around the world?

2. What three things do businesses hope their products' names will do?

3. What does Chris Yaneff say people are really selling when they sell perfume or vodka?

4. What is "positioning"?

5. What word inspired the ad agency to come up with the name "Duracell"?

6. What does the name "Infiniti" suggest?

7. What two characteristics make names successful?

8. What kind of feeling did the name "Swatch" try to give?

9. Give two examples of products from other countries whose names don't work well in North America.

10. Which word in some popular product names such as "Irish Mist" doesn't work well in Germany? Why?

11. How do some companies choose names for their products?

12. Which letter is popular in naming cars?

13. What really counts in a name?

CANADIAN CAPSULES   Many Canadians are familiar with the Pepsi slogan, "Come alive with the Pepsi Generation." When the slogan was used in Taiwan, it was translated as, "Pepsi will bring your ancestors back from the dead."

THE ADVERTISING CAMPAIGN

Project 1

 Look for ads in newspapers and magazines. Bring in examples of some ads that you find. In a group, discuss the ads. Use the descriptions listed below to help you.

1. persuasive
2. irritating
3. offensive
4. informative
5. straightforward
6. silly
7. effective
8. creative

9. appealing to women
10. appealing to men
11. aimed at older people
12. aimed at young children
13. aimed at teenagers
14. racist
15. sexist

Project 2

Work in pairs. Imagine that you work for an advertising agency, and that you are asked to design a campaign for a new product.

1. Choose a product that is interesting to you.

2. Choose a name for your product.

3. Design an ad campaign to promote your product. It can be a newspaper or magazine ad, or it can be a television or radio commercial.

4. Write the slogan or text to accompany the ad. Use visuals, such as photographs or drawings. You can also use music or sound.

5. Present your ad to the class.

If other students want to buy your product, your ad is a success!

IN MY OPINION

The Impact of Advertising

A   Choose one of the topics below, and prepare to debate.

1. Advertising allows consumers to make educated choices when they buy things.

2. Choosing brand names is a reliable way of knowing that you are buying the best products on the market.

3. Advertisements generally present a pretty honest picture of the products they are promoting.

4. Endorsements by famous people guarantee the quality of the products they are promoting.

5. The government should control the kind of advertising that is allowed on television to be sure it isn't misleading.

B   Choose one of the topics to write about. Use information from the unit, as well as your own opinions, to explain your point of view.

SHARPEN YOUR ENGLISH

Pronunciation

A Words with several syllables have primary stress on one syllable. There are different patterns for syllable stress in English. Read the words in each column with your teacher. Then practise saying them with a partner.

First syllable	Second syllable	Second to last syllable
1. télevision	1. detérgent	1. sophisticátion
2. nóticeable	2. succéssful	2. compensátion
3. négative	3. deódorant	3. considerátion
4. víolators	4. persuásive	4. exaggerátion
5. pósitive	5. majórity	5. imitátion
6. réasonable	6. respónsive	6. consultátion
7. sénsible	7. consúltant	7. administrátion
8. pówerful	8. depártment	8. promótion
9. póssible	9. impórtant	9. competítion
10. púrchase	10. endórsements	10. specializátion

B Some related words change the intonation pattern depending on the form of the word. These changes can cause confusion. Practise the pairs of words with your teacher and then with a partner.

1.	anxious	anxiety	6.	department	departmental
2.	advertise	advertisement	7.	experiment	experimental
3.	environment	environmental	8.	government	governmental
4.	commerce	commercial	9.	psychology	psychological
5.	photograph	photographer	10.	vegetable	vegetarian

UNIT 10
MAKING A LIVING

GETTING ALONG AT WORK

A Work in a group of three. Match the two parts of the rules below.

1. If you open it, **close it.**   a) admit it.

2. If you turn it on,   b) don't ask questions.

3. If you unlock it,   c) return it.

4. If you break it,   d) get permission to use it.

5. If you can't fix it,   e) lock it up.

6. If you borrow it,   f) close it.

7. If you value it,   g) call in someone who can.

8. If you make a mess,   h) turn it off.

9. If you move it,   i) leave it alone.

10. If it belongs to someone else,   j) clean it up.

11. If you don't know how to operate it,   k) put it back.

12. If it's none of your business,   l) take care of it.

B Work in your group. Think of items in the workplace that each rule could refer to.

> 1. If you open it, close it.   a filing cabinet, a can of paint

133

C Compare your answers with another group and decide which answers are correct.

> 1. If you open it, close it.   a light ✘
>   (In English you **turn off** a light.)

WHAT'S IMPORTANT IN A JOB?

A Work in a group to discuss these questions.

1. What are the characteristics of a good job?

2. What are the characteristics of a bad job?

3. What is the most interesting job you have ever had?

4. What is the most boring job you have ever had?

5. What would be your ideal job? Why?

B Work together to rank the factors you consider important in a job, from most to least important.

job security

the status of the position

interesting and challenging work

a good salary

long paid vacations

opportunities for travel

possibilities for advancement

benefits (insurance, sick leave, parental leave)

a good boss

nice surroundings

regular working hours

people you enjoy working with

NIGHT WORK

A Work in a group. Read these statements about working at night and decide whether each is true or false.

1. About 20 percent of full-time workers in North America work at night.

2. In the future fewer people will work at night.

3. People's bodies adjust if they work at night over a long period of time.

4. All of these people might be at work during the night: nurses, bankers, journalists, stockbrokers.

5. It is more economical for factories to stay open all night.

6. Night workers lose one night's sleep every week.

7. Night workers drink and smoke less than day workers.

8. Falling asleep on the job is a common problem for night workers.

B   Read the text quickly. Check your answers to the true/false questions.

Night Work

Sandy Bauers

It was 3 a.m. and Milton Hay barely had a moment to chat. While the rest of the world slept peacefully and dreamed sweetly—or so it seemed—Hay was churning out photocopies. He does that all night long. Fridays through Mondays.

He was hardly the only one awake. Milton Hay is just one of 20 million night workers in North America—almost 20 percent of the full-time work force. They not only police our streets, tend our sick and keep our electricity humming, they also transport our goods, monitor our money, entertain us on TV and will sell us a dozen eggs.

Everything seems to be moving to 24-hour mode, from convenience stores to massage parlours. Not even clerical workers go home at 5 p.m. any more. In many cities, support staff at large firms work well into the night. Economists predict the number of people who work "non-standard" schedules will continue to grow as advances in technology link the globe's time zones.

Never mind that night work is bad for your health. Sleep clinics, staffed by yet another group of night workers, have found that even those who have worked nights for years may never get used to it. Their body clocks can't adjust.

Just ask journalist Kevin Coyne. Intrigued by an odd statistic he came across—that at 3 a.m. on any given night, 10 million people in the United States were awake—he decided to look into it.

Most daysiders are unaware of the extent of night work. "If I tell people I work nights, they assume I'm a nurse," a bank employee in Boston told Coyne. Passing the city's big office building at night "they think someone just left the lights on."

Business sees the night as a natural resource—the only one we can't deplete. Tapping the wee hours has spawned a new industry—overnight mail—and altered the financial world. It makes economic sense for a business with expensive equipment to expand operating hours, says a labour economist. Why shell out for the equipment, then let it sit idle for two-thirds of the day? For the price of one operator you can keep a bank of machines whirring all night.

But they are tired. Night workers lose, on average, a full night's worth of sleep every week. Milton Hay, who has a full-time day job as well, says he sleeps only three hours out of every 24—from 7 to 10 p.m. And he manages without coffee. Others are not so lucky. As a group, night workers use more caffeine and other stimulants, drink more alcohol, take more sleeping pills. Everything is magnified if you work a changing shift.

And more than 70 percent of night workers admit they fall asleep on the job every night. Which brings up the issues of job performance and safety. If a trucker zipping along at 90 kilometres an hour or a nuclear power plant operator goes to sleep for even a minute, the results can be deadly.

Yet night work remains largely unstudied. Not even the health effects have been documented. In addition to specific health problems, researchers are concerned about "shift work maladaptation syndrome," a fancy way of saying that people on shift work "feel lousy all the time." You're asking your body to sleep when it wants to be awake, and to stay awake when it wants to sleep. It's similar to jet lag, only it's constant.

Some people want to work the night shift, though. Coyne says it is common in two-career couples with limited child-care options. Some workers say they like the illusion of added time—they can get more chores done during the day. Some are avid golfers. Many enjoy free city parking at night and like not having to buck rush-hour traffic. Few do it for the money, because often there's not enough financial incentive to turn one's life upside down.

By the end of his journey, Coyne developed an affinity for the night time. He found that people were friendlier. They had a healthy disdain for authority and "a willingness to endure adversity." People who work at night, he says "tend to think deeper," because there are fewer distractions. "They have more room and space and freedom to think."

On the other hand, Marty Klein, a psychologist who runs a shift-work consulting firm, imagines life without medical coverage, police, telephone, television, radio, heat, light, water. If we didn't have shift work we'd live from 5 p.m. to 8 a.m. without any of that. Weekends would not be fun. Weekends would be anarchy.

"It's really these people," Klein says, "that make the difference between our modern culture, for all of its pros and cons, vs. literally the Dark Ages."

C Read the text carefully and answer the questions.

1. What kind of work does Milton Hay do?
2. Name five jobs that people do at night.
3. Why do economists predict that the number of night-time jobs will grow in the future?
4. Why do researchers say that working nights is bad for the health?
5. How many people in the United States are awake in the middle of the night?
6. How do businesses view the night?
7. Why does it make economic sense for businesses to operate at night?
8. How much sleep do night workers lose per week?
9. What do many night workers take to manage their lifestyle?
10. Give some examples of situations where disasters can occur if a person falls asleep on the job.
11. Why do many night workers "feel lousy all the time"?
12. Give three reasons why some people like to work at night.
13. What are some characteristics of people who work at night?
14. What services would we not have, if people did not work the night shift?

Sign in a bank in Coquitlam, BC: Due to a shortage of robots, some of our workers are human and may act unpredictably when abused.

STARTING A BUSINESS

 LISTENING ACTIVITY 10   *Interview with Deborah Macklin, Entrepreneur*

A   Discuss these questions.

1.   Do you know anyone who has his or her own business?

2.   What kind of business does this person have?

3.   Have you ever thought about starting a business? If so, what kind?

4.   Where would someone who wanted to start a business begin?

5.   What personal characteristics do you think would contribute to being successful in business?

  B   Read the questions. Then listen to the interview and answer the questions. Use the worksheet.

1.   Why do more and more people want to start their own businesses these days?

2.   When did Deborah first become interested in starting her own business?

3.   What was Deborah asked to do in her job?

4.   What idea did this give her?

5.   Why is it important for a person to know his or her strengths?

6.   Why is it important to find a gap in the market?

7.   What new market needs have opened up in the last few years?

8.   What should you do before you start your own business?

9.   Why is persistence important when you start a business?

10. How long can it take for a business to get off the ground?

11. Why is it important to feel passionate about your business?

12. What two things does Deborah say will help you increase your chances for success?

  C   Work in a group. Imagine that you are about to start your own business. Describe the business and what you would need to get started.

GRAMMAR FOCUS

"Make" and "Do"

Use **make** to give the sense of producing or constructing something concrete. Although the meaning of **make** and **do** is similar, it is not possible to use **do** in the categories of activity below.

a) make clothes

b) make furniture

c) make three-dimensional art and film

d) make manufactured products

e) make food (meals)

A   Match each of the following actions to a category above.

> make spaghetti   **e**

1.	make muffins	11.	make a statue
2.	make dishes	12.	make a pizza
3.	make a sculpture	13.	make a dessert
4.	make a movie	14.	make a dress
5.	make an omelet	15.	make a desk
6.	make cars	16.	make breakfast
7.	make a rocking chair	17.	make a sweater
8.	make a banana cake	18.	make a tool
9.	make a shirt	19.	make a bench
10.	make stuffed animals	20.	make appetizers

The basic meaning of **make** and **do** is the same but each of them combines with particular words and expressions that must be learned by heart.

Make	**Do**
make a mistake	do the dishes
make a speech	do the shopping
make a phone call	do your homework
make an effort	do work
make a decision	do a good job
make love	do the laundry
make war	do the cooking
make noise	do exercise
make an excuse	do well at something
make plans	do badly at something
make reservations	do a favour
make your bed	do your duty
make money	do research
make time	do an assignment
make friends	do your best
make enemies	do a dance
make sense	do yoga
make a deal	do tricks
make a suggestion	do damage
	do good
	do harm

B   Complete the sentences with **make** or **do**.

1.   She _____ yoga every day in order to stay as fit as possible.

2.   Bad eating habits can _____ harm to your health.

3.   The suggestions she _____ are usually excellent ones.

4.   Gaston is friendly and he _____ new friends really easily.

5.   Susan and Maria _____ the same job but Susan is paid more.

6.   The organizers of the Christmas party always _____ a good job.

7.   Their job is to _____ research on the common cold.

8.   Sometimes mother is angry because nobody _____ the dishes.

9.   The politician is famous because he _____ such good speeches.

10. Volunteers generally _____ a lot of money for charity.

C Put the following words in the correct column. Check the list on page 140 if you need help.

research
the dishes
homework
the laundry
a mistake
dinner
an effort
the bed
exercise
a cake
friends
the shopping
a favour
noise
money
enemies
a good job
sense
reservations
yoga
damage
tricks

Make	Do

CANADIAN CAPSULES About three million people in Canada work the night shift, one million Canadians work on Saturdays, and half a million Canadians work on Sundays.

FINDING MONEY

 VIDEO ACTIVITY 6

A   Read the paragraph. Then close your book and write as the teacher dictates.

When you were young and nagged your parents for a new toy or a special treat, they probably responded with the information that money doesn't grow on trees. Since that time you may have dreamed of finding money in the street or marrying a millionaire. More likely, however, you simply resigned yourself to working for a living like the rest of us. Unless of course you managed to win a lottery that set you up for life.

     B   Read the questions with a partner. Then watch the video and answer the questions. Use the worksheet.

1.   How much money is waiting to be claimed?

2.   How does Terry Howes make a living?

3.   How does Mr. Howes look for money?

4.   Describe the case of the Young family.

5.   Why are there so many abandoned bank accounts?

6.   How much money can be in these accounts?

7.   What does Terry Howes look through at the Archives of Ontario?

8.   How far back did the case Howes and Wood cracked go?

9.   When did Christopher Rowe die?

10.   How did the information come to Terry Howes' attention?

11.   How long did the search take?

12.   What had happened to the other family members?

13.   Who was the second Lucretia?

14.   How old is she?

15.   How much money did she get?

16.   What does she treasure the most?

17.   What is Howes' fee for finding money?

18.   Why is it often difficult to persuade people to take money that is found?

19.   What kinds of things have made people today skeptical?

IN MY OPINION

Getting Along at Work

Work in a group to reach a consensus. Rank the importance of these factors in the quality of your workplace, from most to least important.

the smoking policy

the amount of privacy

the colour of the walls

the source of lighting

the amount of noise

the reliability of equipment you use

relations with your co-workers

safety features on the work site

Your Co-Workers

Work in a group. Try to find solutions to the following situations.

Situation A

You depend on a photocopy machine to do your job. Frequently, when you go to the photocopy room, all of the machines are down. Sometimes the machines are out of paper. Sometimes there are paper jams that haven't been cleared. Sometimes there are mechanical or electrical problems. Whenever you ask for help, the person you have asked says he or she isn't responsible for the problem. You are tired of these shirkers. What is the solution?

Situation B

You work with someone who is a gossip. During coffee breaks in the cafeteria, he is always very friendly and asks a lot of questions. The next thing you know, you hear your personal information being repeated by others. It's very hard to avoid this man because you work together. Sometimes you notice that he seems to be listening to your private phone conversations. You don't like your personal life to be the subject of gossip. What can you do?

Situation C

One of your co-workers is a sponger. She's always asking to borrow your stapler or pencil sharpener or some office supplies. She usually forgets to return things she has borrowed. When she has a cold, she uses up all your tissues and doesn't replace the box. The worst thing is that she is always asking for a few dollars until pay day. When you ask for the money back she always acts surprised and annoyed. You don't want bad relations with someone you work with. What is the best solution?

SHARPEN YOUR ENGLISH

Vocabulary

A   Here are some personality types you may meet in the workplace. Work in a group and discuss the meaning of each term on the left. Match the terms for personality types to the descriptions on the right.

Personality Types	**Descriptions**
1. a shirker	a) someone who talks about others behind their backs
2. a gossip	
3. a procrastinator	b) someone who never gets around to doing things
4. a show-off	
5. a sponger	c) someone who reports people to the boss
6. a blabbermouth	d) someone who always borrows money or things
7. a workaholic	
8. a tattle-tale	e) someone who always wants everyone's attention
	f) someone who talks a lot
	g) someone who has no interests outside of work
	h) someone who always tries to pass on their work to others

B Here are some famous adages (wise sayings) that are used in English. First match each saying to a personality type in Exercise A. Then discuss the kind of advice you could give each of the personality types.

1. Never put off until tomorrow what you can do today.

2. Neither a borrower nor a lender be, for loan oft loses both itself and friend. (Shakespeare)

3. Better to stay silent and be thought a fool, than to open your mouth and prove it. (Disraeli)

4. All work and no play, makes Jack a dull boy (or Jill a dull girl).

5. People who live in glass houses shouldn't throw stones.

6. An empty vessel makes the most noise.

7. Remember that a person who will tell you something bad about someone will surely tell someone something bad about you.

8. A person saying it can't be done shouldn't interrupt a person who is doing it. (Confucius)

Community Contact Task 1

In Class

Work in a group. Make a list of grocery stores or markets in your area. Divide into pairs. Decide which store each pair of students will visit.

In the Community

With your partner, do a survey of new or unusual foods in the store. Ask questions in the store whenever possible (for example, at the meat or cheese counter, at the in-store demonstrations, etc.). If possible, bring in samples of the foods to share with the class. Look for foods in the categories below:

1. convenience, or ready-made foods

2. specialty foods (oils, vinegars)

3. imported packaged foods

4. spices, sauces, and marinades

5. baked goods

6. exotic fruits and vegetables

Reporting Back

Work in your group again. Share your information.

Community Contact Task 2

In Class

In a small group, prepare a list of items that you would enclose in a time capsule, to show future generations what is "hot," or in style today.

Discuss which items would best represent the current fashion in the following categories:

1. clothing for women and men

2. hairstyles

3. shoe fashions

4. music

5. movies

6. TV shows

7. leisure activities

In the Community

Draw or find pictures or examples for each category. Write a short paragraph to describe each item.

Reporting Back

Compare the different time capsules in the class.

148

Community Contact Task 3

In Class

Work in groups. Choose a type of animal (for example, birds) or a region of the world (for example, Australia). List several types of animals in your category or region.

In the Community

1. In pairs, go to a library. Find out which animals on your list are in danger of extinction. Find out why these animals are in danger, and what, if anything, is being done to save them.

2. Discuss other ways you can get information about endangered animals. For example, you can call or visit a zoo or consult wildlife experts and animal preservation groups in your community.

3. With your partner, prepare a report on the animals you researched.

Reporting Back

Present your report to the class. You may want to decide on a plan of action to save one animal or group of animals (for example, contribute to a fund or "adopt" an animal at the zoo).

Community Contact Task 4

In Class

Work in a group. Make a list of common superstitions.

In the Community

Survey people from different cultural backgrounds about their superstitions. Put their ideas and information in the chart. Use the worksheet.

	Person A	Person B	Person C
a good luck sign			
a bad luck sign			
a lucky number			
an unlucky number			
a lucky piece of clothing or jewelry			
a superstition about food			
a superstition about an animal			
a superstition about the weather			

Reporting Back

In your group, compare information. How many superstitions from your original list appeared on your chart?

Community Contact Task 5

In Class

Work in groups. Make a list of common illnesses or problems people have (for example, a cold, a rash). Then make a list of things people in your group do for the conditions. Describe any home remedies used, or who would be consulted for help.

In the Community

Survey people from different cultural backgrounds about how they would deal with the conditions on your list. Make a chart, and put the information into the chart.

Reporting Back

Share your information. How do treatments used in the community compare with the treatments used by people in the class?

Community Contact Task 6

In Class

Work in groups. Write questions to ask people in your community about their rites of passage. Follow the examples below and add other questions of your own.

1. Is there a celebration in your culture for becoming an adult?

2. What is the best age to get married and have children?

3. What is the best age to move out of your parents' home?

4. What makes a person feel like an adult?

In the Community

Survey people of different ages and from different cultural backgrounds. Ask the questions on your list.

Reporting Back

Share your information.

Community Contact Task 7

In Class

Work in groups. Make a list of name-brand products in the categories listed below.

Name brands	
laundry detergent	
soup	
orange juice	
spaghetti sauce	
crackers	
mustard	
potato chips	
coffee	
yogurt	
cheese	

In the Community

In pairs, go to a large supermarket.

1. Look for the items listed. How many name brands do you see from your list? How many other brands do you see? Add them to your chart.

2. Observe the shoppers. How many of them buy the most popular name brands? How many buy the less popular, or no-name brands? Put a check (✔) every time you see someone buy a name-brand item from your list. Put an ✗ beside the item when you see someone buy an unadvertised or no-name product.

Reporting Back

Share your information with the class.

Community Contact Task 8

In Class

Work in a group.

1. Make a list of occupations that people do at night.

2. Write questions to ask people who work at night. Aim to find out what the people do in their jobs and how they feel about their work.

In the Community

Work with a partner. Interview two people who work at night. Ask your questions. Get as many details as you can.

Reporting Back

Work in a group. Share your information.

Appendix: Irregular Verbs

Many past participles are the same as the regular or irregular past tense forms. Irregular past participles are shown in bold type below.

Present	Past	Past participle
arise	arose	**arisen**
awake	awoke	**awaken**
be	was, were	**been**
beat	beat	**beaten**
become	became	**become**
begin	began	**begun**
bite	bit	**bitten**
bleed	bled	bled
blow	blew	**blown**
break	broke	**broken**
bring	brought	brought
build	built	built
buy	bought	bought
catch	caught	caught
choose	chose	**chosen**
come	came	**come**
cost	cost	cost
cut	cut	cut
dig	dug	dug
do	did	**done**
draw	drew	**drawn**
drink	drank	**drunk**
drive	drove	**driven**
eat	ate	**eaten**
fall	fell	**fallen**
feed	fed	fed
feel	felt	felt
find	found	found
fly	flew	**flown**
forbid	forbade	**forbidden**
forget	forgot	**forgotten**
forgive	forgave	**forgiven**
freeze	froze	**frozen**
get	got	**gotten** (got)
give	gave	**given**
go	went	**gone**
grow	grew	**grown**
have	had	had
hear	heard	heard
hide	hid	**hidden**
hit	hit	hit

Present	Past	Past participle
hold	held	held
hurt	hurt	hurt
keep	kept	kept
know	knew	**known**
lay	laid	laid
lead	led	led
leave	left	left
let	let	let
lie	lay	**lain**
lose	lost	lost
make	made	made
mean	meant	meant
meet	met	met
pay	paid	paid
put	put	put
read	read	read
ride	rode	**ridden**
ring	rang	**rung**
rise	rose	**risen**
run	ran	**ran**
see	saw	**seen**
sell	sold	sold
send	sent	sent
shake	shook	**shaken**
shine	shone	shone
shoot	shot	shot
show	showed	shown
shrink	shrank	**shrunk**
shut	shut	shut
sing	sang	**sung**
sit	sat	sat
sleep	slept	slept
speak	spoke	**spoken**
spread	spread	spread
spring	sprang	**sprung**
stand	stood	stood
steal	stole	**stolen**
stink	stank	**stunk**
swear	swore	**sworn**
swim	swam	**swum**
take	took	taken
teach	taught	taught
tear	tore	**torn**
tell	told	told
think	thought	thought
throw	threw	**thrown**
understand	understood	understood
wake	woke	**woken**
wear	wore	**worn**
win	won	won
write	wrote	**written**

Englisch ist einfach

ben englizce oranmak stiurum

私は英語が好きです.

أنا أحب هذا الكتاب

Saya suka buku ini

Bu Kitapi cok seudim

我會說英文

See you in Canadian Concepts 6!

Delam mikhad englisi yad begiram

Mi piace molto questo libro

Tôi thích quyển sách này

Inglês é fácil de aprender.

Je parle l'anglais

안녕

私はこの本が大好きです.

Mijaw Egguvuá

ME GUSTA HABLAR INGLES

Mou' αρέσει αυτό τό Βιβλίο

157